NO VIVALDI IN THE GARAGE

ADVISOR IN MUSIC TO NORTHEASTERN UNIVERSITY PRESS
Gunther Schuller

No Vivaldi in the Garage

A REQUIEM FOR
CLASSICAL MUSIC
IN NORTH AMERICA

Sheldon Morgenstern

Northeastern University Press
Boston
Published by University Press of New England
Hanover and London

NORTHEASTERN UNIVERSITY PRESS
Published by University Press of New England,
One Court Street, Lebanon, NH 03766
www.upne.com

First Northeastern University Press/UPNE paperback edition 2005
Printed in the United States of America   5   4   3   2   1

ISBNs for the paperback edition:
    ISBN-13: 9781555536411
    ISBN-10: 1-55553-641-7

Library of Congress Cataloging-in-Publication Data
Morgenstern, Sheldon.
     No Vivaldi in the Garage : a requiem for classical music in North America /
Sheldon Morgenstern.
        p. cm.
     Includes bibliographical entries (p.) and index.
     ISBN 1-55553-493-7 (cloth : alk. paper)
     1. Morgenstern, Sheldon. 2. Conductors (Music)—United States—Biography.
3. Music—Social Aspects—North America. I. Title.

ML422.M737 A3 2001
784.2′092—dc01
[B 21; aa05 05-21]   2001026625

Dedicated to the memories of
Leonard Rose and
Josef Gingold

CONTENTS

In a 1963 speech at Amherst College, John F. Kennedy said:

> I see little of more importance to the future of our country and our
> civilization than full recognition of the place of the artist. If art is to
> nourish the roots of our culture, society must set the artist free to
> follow his vision wherever it takes him. Art is not a form of propa-
> ganda, it is a form of truth and establishes the basic human truths
> which must serve as the touchstones of our judgment.

In the 1995 film Mr. Holland's Opus, *there is an informative and important dialogue between Mr. Holland, who is the school's orchestra conductor,
and the principal, Gene, who has been instructed to make budget cuts.*

> GENE: I care about these kids just as much as you do, but if I'm
> forced to choose between Mozart and reading and writing and long
> division, I choose long division.

> MR. HOLLAND: Well, you can cut the arts as much as you want,
> Gene, but sooner or later these kids aren't going to have anything to
> read or write about.

PREFACE

ALTHOUGH I NOW LIVE IN FRANCE, HARDLY A WEEK GOES by without my receiving bad news from Canada or the United States. A former student or colleague has been dismissed from a teaching position because a college/university/conservatory has decided it can no longer afford all the teachers in its music program. Or a symphony orchestra has shut down, throwing ninety or more people, many of them my personal friends, out of work.

I receive such news with great sadness, and increasingly I have trouble finding words of encouragement to counter the despair I feel. Being a professional orchestral musician requires years of single-minded devotion to music, and the financial rewards—when one is fortunate enough to find a job—are rarely commensurate with the cost of schooling, paying for private lessons, and purchasing a fine instrument.

Since the initial publication of this book, the orchestras in San Jose, Tulsa, Winnipeg, Boca Raton, Cleveland (Ohio Chamber Orchestra), San Antonio, Colorado Springs, Savannah, Calgary, and Fort Lauderdale, as well as the Montana Music Festival, have declared bankruptcy. Meanwhile, the orchestras in Toronto, Brooklyn, Rochester, St. Louis, Charlotte, Houston, Pittsburgh, and Phoenix came perilously close to the same fate and still are not out of the woods. Other orchestras that have suffered enormous financial losses include those in Detroit, Vancouver, Milwaukee, Baltimore, Houston, Montreal, and Chicago. And this list is surely partial, given that it includes only those organizations willing to go public about their problems. As Bernard Holland wrote in the *New York Times* on July 2, 2003, "Even musical fortresses like the Pittsburgh Symphony and the Chicago Symphony are, by all reports, leaking blood by the quart."

My conducting and teaching career has spanned four decades of tremendous change, and I have spent my adult life encouraging young people to pursue careers in music. Was I wrong to? Would they have been better off without my stoking dreams that are so out of step with present realities?

Perhaps. But the realities present such an ugly contrast with what might be—what still can be if those in positions of power would recognize the vital importance of arts education in our public schools and step up governmental funding to a serious level—that I feel compelled to speak. This book is my attempt to give voice to the great passion I still feel for classical music, the love I have for my former students and colleagues, and the indignation I feel at what is happening to all three. I hope it will be read as a call for change—before it is too late.

In the April 21, 2003, issue of the *New Yorker,* there is a cartoon that depicts a group of Neanderthals posing the following question to their elders: "Why are the arts always the first thing to be cut, when you know damn well it's the only thing that separates us from the monkeys?"

Spring 2005

ACKNOWLEDGMENTS

IN ADDITION TO THE NORTH AMERICAN ORCHESTRAL STAFF members who assisted by completing the questionnaire reproduced in Appendix 1, I wish to thank the many musicians and other friends who gave valuable time in reading drafts and helping me obtain factual information. My sincere appreciation to Pete Bradshaw, Neal Cary, Gregory Cox, Nancy Dawson-Sauser, Michael Dreyfuss, Cary Ebli, Daniel Grosgurin, Sali and Jonathan Hagan, Don Harry, James Jenkins, Lisa Johnson, James Lambert, Gail LeBauer, Renée Leroux-Ward, Kathryn Logan, Selby McPhee, James Newlin, Frederik Prausnitz, Carl Roskott, Robert Roth, Ann Schein, Rebecca Siegel, Ömer Sipahi, Paula and Lee Swepston, Jeanne Tannenbaum, Wendy Vactor, Nancy Wannamaker, Ursula Warren, James Weissman, and Elizabeth Wheaton.

No Vivaldi in the Garage would never have been possible without the encouragement, guidance, prodding, and determination of my long-time friends Norma McLemore and Tom Huey, and especially the patience of my wife, Patsy, whom I married in Geneva in 1991. She has had much experience editing for international and scholarly organizations, and many were the days when I heard from her, "The last part of this chapter is a mess. I don't have the foggiest idea what you're trying to say. Go to a café and think about it. And please bring a baguette home for dinner."

Patsy also made the suggestion that I offer the reader my list of favorite compositions by genre, and I am pleased to do so.

Symphony: Beethoven's Symphony No. 7
Concerto: Beethoven's Piano Concerto No. 4
Solo work for any instrument: J. S. Bach's *Goldberg Variations*
Composition for string orchestra: *Divertimento* by that blasted Bartók.

NO VIVALDI IN THE GARAGE

ONE

First Notes

THERE IS NO SWEETER SOUND THAN THE SWISH OF A BASKET-
ball going through the net—with the possible exception of Ella Fitzger-
ald singing "Mack the Knife." But even she doesn't bring me to tears the
way that *Judas Maccabaeus* did the first time I heard it performed.

It was 1965. I had just been named an assistant conductor at the New
England Conservatory of Music (NEC) when the West German Ministry of Culture invited major music schools in the United States to send
delegates for the purpose of exchanging educational concepts. Because
NEC's conductor, Fred Prausnitz, was not available and the dean was
not a musician, the administration decided to send me. The rest of the
group were the deans from the University of Michigan, Indiana University, the Eastman School of Music, and the Juilliard School. We met
with colleagues in Bonn, Munich, Cologne, and Berlin, and the discussions often turned to what was then a serious and continuing problem
for German orchestras. They had lost their Jewish musicians and were
finding it difficult to train a new generation to fill the ranks of their ensembles and music schools.

About an hour's drive from Munich was a small village (the name of which I have long forgotten) that imported several productions each year. Gid Waldrop, who was dean of the Juilliard School and who became a very good friend, asked me if I would go there with him the next day to hear an orchestra and chorus, conducted by the great Karl Richter, perform Handel's *Judas Maccabaeus*. The others in our group were not interested, so Gid and I rented a car, drove to the village, and easily found the church.

When we arrived we saw no coats, ties, or fancy dresses, but country folk, many farmers and their families, who filled every inch of space in a small church that was relatively new, clearly built after the end of the Second World War. We arrived later than planned, and about five minutes before the concert began one of the young ushers found us two old wooden folding chairs. But the uncomfortable arrangement (*Judas Maccabaeus* lasts close to two hours) didn't matter once the program began.

I don't think that anyone who has such an experience can pinpoint exactly how the ingredients make it so special. Was it the six wonderful vocal soloists, the lovely sound of the organ, the fact that I had never before heard *Judas Maccabaeus* in a live setting, the tone colors of the Munich Chamber Orchestra, the fact that no audience member seemed to move for two hours, the genius of Richter, who conducted with unbelievable pacing and nuance? As the two horns played their glorious duet near the end, I realized that for me it was a combination of these factors that resulted in absolute magic. It was and remains the most profound artistic experience of my life.

When the concert was over I began to cry, and the teenage usher stayed with me for nearly five minutes to be certain I was okay. Afterward I found Gid outside and could see that his eyes were also red. We didn't speak on the trip back to Munich.

◙ I WAS BORN IN JULY 1938 IN CLEVELAND, OHIO. EARLY ON, I thought of Cleveland as belonging to Artur Rodzinski because he was music director of the Cleveland Orchestra, which was then, and arguably still is, the world's greatest symphony orchestra, located right there in middle America. The day after my birth my paternal grandfather came to see me, went home, and died of a heart attack. This became a great family joke—"All it took was one look at you"—a joke that I alone never appreciated.

I have mostly fond memories of my six Cleveland years, and I especially recall being surrounded by classical music and hearing boisterous discussions about sports events. My uncle Morty, who had worked his way through medical school as concertmaster of the Louisville Symphony, was the unofficial team doctor for the Cleveland Indians. What an incredible moment for a five-year-old: to go into the locker room and actually talk to his heroes! I even had Hall of Fame pitcher Bob Feller and shortstop Lou Boudreau autograph my baseballs. Years later I discovered that Boudreau, the youngest player/manager in the history of the sport, had obtained his college degree in music from Northwestern University, just as I did sixteen years later.

The great cellist Leonard Rose lived just down the street from us and gave lessons to my young cousin, Zoe, newly arrived from Poland. She was on one of the last ships to leave in 1938 just before the Nazi invasion. Her mother was ill, and the United States Immigration Service didn't allow sick emigrants to board the ships. Zoe never saw her again. Several of my family members got to Cleveland this way, but most of those left behind didn't survive the war.

My paternal grandmother, Sali, was born and reared in what was then the small and quiet village of Auschwitz, Poland, before immigrating to the United States in 1899 as a newlywed. When she was pregnant with her eldest child, Fan (who later became the first female member of the Cleveland Orchestra), she returned to her home city to give birth, a tradition in those days. Afterward she immediately came back to Cleveland. Many times in my youth I asked my father, Irwin, about the birthplaces of Mama Sali, as we called her, and Grandpa Sam. The answer was always "I'm not really certain but I think it was Austria." It was a reply I never accepted. How can anyone not know the birthplaces of his or her parents? I discovered the answer years later when I was living in Geneva, Switzerland. A great-uncle, Sig Halbreich, who lives in California, sent me a copy of his book about how he survived five Nazi concentration camps, the last being Auschwitz, which was about twenty kilometers from his birthplace. In his book he included some grainy

5

family reunion photos taken early in the century in the village of Auschwitz. I was dumbfounded to find my grandparents in those photos. In a later visit to Geneva, Sig explained to me that in many large North American cities there was at that time (and in some cities still is) a "pecking order" among immigrant Jews. Those from Germany, France, and Austria were socially at the top, those from Hungary in the middle, with Romanians, Czechoslovakians, Russians, and Poles being the outcasts. Being Polish was simply too embarrassing to admit, even to their children.

My father was a strapping six-foot, two-inch, young man. Each weekend he and some friends would look in the *Plain Dealer* (Cleveland's main newspaper) for weddings that were taking place. They would put on their best suits, go to the church or synagogue, and simply say to the usher, "I'm with the bride's family" or "I'm with the groom's family"; after the ceremony, in they'd go to the reception for free food and drink and, best of all, a dance with the young women. It was at one of these weddings that he cut in to dance with my mother, whom he had never seen before.

Harriet, a petite, dark-haired beauty, was a gifted young pianist who as a teenager often played for radio broadcasts. She was swept off her feet by my father, who was then selling furniture and playing semiprofessional basketball, and she married him when she was seventeen, after two years of college as a music major. She became a traditional housewife, never again to return to her art professionally. She spent much of her life encouraging me to become a musician and to appreciate her support for such causes as women's rights, as well as her opposition to war and the death penalty. Years later she marched in demonstrations against our involvement in Vietnam and worked in the presidential campaigns of Eugene McCarthy and George McGovern (to my father's horror, but my delight). Before we moved away from Cleveland, my mother had already started giving piano lessons to my sister, Judy, and me, and the family made regular weekly trips to Severance Hall to hear the Cleveland Orchestra and visiting soloists.

One night when I was five we went to hear the great pianist Alexander Brailowsky in an all-Chopin recital. We had scratchy recordings of him at home, but I wasn't prepared for his swooping phrases, technical facility, and powerful playing. Nor was I prepared to hear the ushers yelling loudly, "Bravo!" Hearing Brailowsky in a live performance was a turning point in my life. I knew I wanted to become a musician and was so overwhelmed by this ambition that the next morning, a Saturday, my parents had to drag me away from the piano.

My father and I often saw Indians' games at Memorial Stadium, and I loved watching my uncle Morty in the dugout while I was eating as many hot dogs as I could stomach. In between bites I'd yell such intelligent suggestions as "Kill the ump!" and "Brush him back, Feller!"— what insiders call "chin music."

The worst experience I had in Cleveland took place during a day I had greatly looked forward to. My father had taken me to the Euclid Beach Amusement Park. While we were riding the Ferris wheel it shuddered and stopped, stranding us at the very top for what felt like years. Even the most attentive parents cannot always provide security for their children. My fear of heights continues to this day. I refuse to drive on aqueducts in Europe, and I also make certain that my contract specifies a rail around the podium wherever I am asked to guest conduct. I also use steps or elevators rather than escalators whenever possible. I can rationalize air travel as something not to be feared because once I've boarded it's all in the hands of the pilot and out of my control. I do, however, say a short silent prayer before each takeoff and landing.

Because of serious pains in his legs my father had tests done, first at the Cleveland Clinic and then at Johns Hopkins, where the doctors told him that his pains were caused by smoking, which he had never even tried. They then told him to move to a warmer climate. So the family moved to Greensboro, North Carolina, just after I had started grammar school. They chose the city because it was a short drive to High Point, "The Furniture Capital of the World," which suited my father's line of work. Also, we had relatives in the area, and the winters were not so severe as in Ohio. My mother decided it would be better for me to have a trained piano teacher, so I continued lessons with my aunt Sandy LeBauer. Soon a basketball hoop appeared in our backyard. My daily routine was school, back home for piano practice, and finally outside for shooting hoops with neighborhood friends and even my father, when he was in town.

We joined the Jewish temple in Greensboro, although we seldom attended services other than those held on major religious holidays. I never felt any particular ethnic identity, and the fact that there was a war raging in Europe that was claiming the lives of so many of our relatives was not discussed at home.

The only member of my extended family who ever made a great deal of money in the arts was my father's second cousin, Freddie Morgan. Freddie was the first of the Morgenstern clan to anglicize his last name; all the others, except for my father, brother, and me, eventually did so. Freddie had written two pop ballads that had become famous and were near the top of the list for 45 rpm sales for years. One was "Sayonara," the other, "Hey, Mister Banjo." The reason he gave for the name change was that the record company couldn't get his full name on the 45s because of the limited space.

Freddie's real money came from his years as the guitarist in the Spike Jones Band. Shortly after our family had moved to Greensboro, Spike's band came through on tour, and my sister and I became the envy of all our friends when we bragged about our cousin Freddie. Freddie's main role was in an act in which he played one of the students in Spike's classroom. Freddie would start shifting around and finally grab his crotch, each time raising his hand to ask the teacher a question, only to be rebuffed. When the teacher finally said, "Okay, Freddie, what's your problem?" Freddie gave an audible sigh of relief and said, "Nothing any longer, sir." It was risqué for the times and always brought great laughs from the crowd.

During their gig in Greensboro, in one of their most famous acts, which dealt with a horse race, Freddie got Spike to substitute my name and my sister's for the names of two of the horses. We were in heaven — and even more so after the show, when Freddie brought the band to our modest home for drinks, food, and nonsense. My mother finally kicked them all out (along with family friends) when one band member was determined to show everyone that he could juggle five eggs at once, only to discover that of course he couldn't; it was the gin speaking.

When I was eleven I played a piano recital in a large hall in Greensboro and afterward was approached by the band director of both my junior high school and the largest senior high school in town. He said that someone with my talent must learn to perform on another instrument and join his band. This led to a strange series of circumstances that profoundly affected my music career. My father took me to a local music store, where we tried to rent a flute, only to find that they had none in stock, but the friendly saleswoman suggested the saxophone and promised to have it delivered that evening. She did carry out the delivery promise, but the instrument turned out to be a trumpet. (There were no saxophones in stock, either.) After a few months the band director asked if I would agree to switch to the French horn, since there were plenty of other students on trumpet, and he guaranteed that I would be promoted to the senior band immediately. I refused. I didn't want to play the horn (as classical musicians refer to the French horn). Learning to play the trumpet is relatively easy for a beginner, and I knew the horn was far more difficult. Each week the director held auditions for promotion and although I was always completely prepared, I was never promoted. Meanwhile I listened to others with less talent who had moved up to the senior band. Finally, I gave up the fight, and horn it was at age twelve.

While I was attempting to become proficient on the horn, basketball was becoming increasingly important to me, and I was the only eighth grader to make the junior high school varsity team. I wasn't quick or a good jumper but I loved making assists and could shoot, the quintessential winner at the game of "H-O-R-S-E." When I was invited to play on an all-city team in the statewide contest, I flipped. We did well, winning three in a row to get to the finals. It was an exciting final game, although we eventually lost to a team from Charlotte. After the game some official person was presenting to a teammate and me (we were co-captains) the bronze runner-up trophy of a man holding a basketball— when its head fell off! I was the only one who thought it funny. Our coach was furious and told me that you weren't supposed to laugh at *anything* when you lose a game. Ever.

When I entered high school I had my first experience playing in an orchestra. What a revelation it was to play with string players such works as Tchaikovsky's Symphony No. 4 and some of the Mozart Symphonies (Nos. 35 and 40) that have treacherous horn parts. I'll never forget the blending of winds and strings at the first rehearsal. Hearing an orchestra is one thing, participating in one for the first time quite another. What a thrill for me to be able to play my own part in a seventy-five-piece ensemble that was rehearsing great compositions that I had previously heard only on recordings or in concert halls. Because of its five string sections, an orchestra's sound is far richer than a band's. No wonder the great composers wrote 99.9 percent of their works, excluding solo and chamber music, for symphony orchestras.

My musical life began to get complicated when the band director took aim at the orchestra conductor and determined to control the school music program, deciding when and if he would allow the wind, brass, and percussion students to be released from band two days a week to rehearse with the orchestra. Basketball practices also presented scheduling conflicts. I did start the first game on the junior varsity in the tenth grade, but I was soon faced with having orchestra rehearsals and basketball practice at the same time once each week.

Choosing which activity to give up was influenced by other factors, not the least of which was talent. The fact of the matter was that, except in ability, I was not unlike former Wake Forest University player Billy Packer, about whom his coach, Bones McKinney, once said: "When Billy got the ball in his hands he wouldn't pass it to his grandmother if he thought he might be able to get a shot off." And so I decided that basketball had to go at the beginning of the following year: average point guards who are "gunners" are a dime a dozen, while good French horn players are rare. In my last game, against a team from the neighboring town of Burlington, the score was tied and our coach called a timeout with minutes to go. In the huddle I was instructed to immediately get the ball inside to our tallest player. Instead I shot, missed, shot, and missed again as time ran out before the coach could yank me. Somehow we won anyway.

Before finishing the tenth grade I decided it would be a good idea to attend a summer music festival. There were few possibilities—Tanglewood and Aspen accepted only older students at the time, and I had heard from teachers and friends that Interlochen not only was fraught with unnecessary competition but also required all students to wear uniforms. That left only Brevard, located in the mountains of North Carolina. Brevard offered me a full scholarship—I thought. When I arrived I was told that I actually had a work scholarship and that three times a week I would be required to shovel rock from a truck onto the road that circled their lake. Because it rains at least every other day in the mountains of North Carolina, the work was endless and backbreaking. I felt

I'd sold my soul to the company store just to have the opportunity to play great music.

For my own improvement and orchestral experience I returned to Brevard the following two summers. I eventually got my work scholarship assignment changed to selling ice cream and candy at the concession. How I loved those Nutty Buddies I stole after closing the store on concert evenings when I wasn't performing!

It wasn't long before I realized in my first summer there that Brevard existed largely for the benefit and aggrandizement of its founder and music director, Jim Pfohl. Jim was the epitome of the Music Man, a great hustler but a near-disaster as a conductor. As the founder of the Brevard Festival, he used his position to con almost everyone he came in contact with, raising money for it in much the same way an evangelical preacher dupes thousands and converts them to his cause.

As a fund-raiser, Pfohl traveled throughout the South in hopes of getting large donations. After his travels he brought expensive gifts back to selected staff members, and it was openly assumed that all the donations weren't reflected in the budget. His personal assistant, a trombonist named Jeff Tate who was a true southerner from Georgia with an authentic accent to match, years later described to me life on the road with Pfohl. They would travel from city to city to meet with women's clubs, presenting their dog and pony routine just before the cucumber sandwiches and tea were served. According to Jeff, he and Jim would wait in whatever pantry was available until they were asked to give their talks, at which time Jim would pull from his coat a flask filled with bourbon, take a few hefty swigs, and say, "Okay, Boy, let's go get 'em."

Jim would speak first, talk a bit about the program and what it meant to the students who had never before had such an experience, build it to a fever pitch, even choking up a little, and then say to my friend, "I simply can't go on. Boy, you take it from here." Jeff's words were something along the lines of how Brevard and dear Dr. Pfohl had given him the opportunity to see the mountaintop, that were it not for Pfohl only the Lord knows what might have happened to him, blah, blah. And the women couldn't get out their checkbooks fast enough. Jeff told me that although he traveled with Jim for months he wasn't certain that Pfohl ever knew his actual name because in all their conversations he was referred to only as "Boy." Still, Pfohl treated him well enough. Jeff told me that the better the take, the better the steak at dinner that evening.

Eventually, Jim got caught with his hand in the cookie jar and was dismissed in 1966, when I was already a professional conductor. In spite of all his faults, what he created for me and many students should not be forgotten. He may have been close to a musical fraud but he did offer an opportunity for gifted young musicians to pursue their dreams. He provided a setting that inspired many of us to pursue solid professional careers in the symphony orchestra field.

For my first concert with him we played the Tchaikovsky Symphony No. 4, and I was in seventh heaven. The other students, especially the strings, were excellent, and each rehearsal was special to me. Pfohl would stop from time to time to talk about his thoughts of the babbling brooks and the wind rippling through the trees, but he never said anything really constructive, such as who was out of tune or how he thought a certain passage should be phrased. Yet few seemed to mind—music-making was *the* issue for us, and we did our best despite him.

Pfohl's conducting assistant was Bob Hause, a fine musician. Bob once told me that Jim gave him the scores for upcoming rehearsals with instructions to write in cues and bowings before handing them back. (Bowings are the direction in which string players move the bow, up or down, to achieve the intent of the composer. Cues are for entrances for the musicians, and are especially important for those who have not played for several minutes, such as a tuba or timpani player.) That Jim was not able to do his own bowings is, I suppose, understandable. In any case, this should be the job of the concertmaster and the other principal strings. But cues? Any first-year conducting student should know how to do that. When Bob was once asked to cover a rehearsal he discovered such handwritten comments in Jim's scores as "Stop here, talk about moon shadows," "Stop here, tell joke."

Each summer we had one guest conductor, Thor Johnson, who was then the music director of the Cincinnati Symphony. We thought Thor was a great conductor, and everyone was excited during his week of rehearsals and concert. It took me five years to realize that Thor was only an adequate conductor and Jim was little better than incompetent.

One teacher at Brevard was excellent by any standards. My horn teacher there was Bob Elworthy, perhaps the most accurate North American player of that treacherously difficult instrument. He was also a first-class and thoughtful teacher. Bob was then principal horn in the New Orleans Philharmonic and later assumed the same position in the Minnesota Orchestra.

During those three summers I made friends who helped me in many ways later on—fellow students who, after a few years, joined me in the professional world, and soloists such as Ivan Davis and Leonard Pennario, who each appeared later as guest artists at the Eastern Music Festival. My accomplishments at Brevard included regular Ping-Pong victories, there being no basketball hoops at the site. I was also named a Concerto Competition Winner and Outstanding Musician during my last summer. However, no one should be misled. I was never a truly outstanding horn player or a natural talent on the instrument. Unlike many others, I had to work day in and day out to remain a more than competent player. I envied those musicians who were able to go days without touching their instruments while I had to play absolutely every day to avoid disastrous performances. If I missed a day, I felt that I was nearly starting from scratch. My range would decrease and I had difficulty getting notes to "speak." I had become a partial slave to my instrument.

During my junior and senior years in high school I was principal horn in the North Carolina All-State Orchestra and continued piano lessons at the University of North Carolina at Greensboro (UNC–G). I received an award at graduation ceremonies—The Most Likely to Succeed in Chosen Profession. The award turned out to be a fiasco, much like my decapitated basketball trophy. That superlative carried with it a fifty-dollar prize, which was to be presented by the treasurer of the area musicians' union, who, I later was told, was an important drug dealer. When I got to the stage to receive the check the union official whispered to me, "I forgot the check, so please pretend that it's in this envelope I'm going to give you." Afterward he told me that it would be mailed to me the following week. It's still in the mail.

During my senior year in high school, 1956, I was given several opportunities to conduct student groups. I had some experience in dealing with the conductor's scores because Bob Elworthy at Brevard had told me at my first lesson, "You can't simply play the notes, you *must* look at the

13

conductor's score to learn how your part fits into the entire picture." I must have impressed someone because I was asked to rehearse the Bee-thoven Symphony No. 8 with the UNC–G Orchestra for two days. More than pride, I felt elation at being able to convey my concepts of music-making to a full orchestra. Playing in a symphony orchestra is quite different from being able to shape the music as a conductor. The conducting bug was beginning to take hold!

But at that time conducting had to take a backseat to playing. Our high school orchestra was invited to perform at the National Music Educators Conference in St. Louis, and the program included Wagner's *Seigfried's Rhine Journey,* which features one of the most difficult horn solos ever written. Somehow I pulled it off with only a few bobbles and afterward was approached by a Northwestern University (NU) professor who of-fered me a full scholarship to attend that school. I accepted on the spot, with the condition that I be allowed to have a double major in horn and conducting. At that time it seemed like a dream come true—their horn teacher, who was principal horn in the Chicago Symphony, was *the* American horn player and teacher, Philip Farkas. The teacher of con-ducting and director of the NU Symphony Orchestra was none other than Thor Johnson.

Academic bureaucracy intervened. I received a letter from the NU Admissions Department in June of that year informing me that because I had never taken the SATs I could not be admitted for the coming school year, but they would hold the scholarship for me in the event I wanted to choose another school and then transfer. Through the efforts of Elworthy, I was given the same arrangement (except for the conduct-ing study possibilities) at Florida State University (FSU). FSU had at that time the finest school of music in the southeastern United States, a reputation that continues today. With few exceptions my time at FSU was largely uneventful.

Ernst von Dohnányi, the wonderful Hungarian composer and con-ductor, was on the faculty. Dohnányi had somehow survived the Nazi re-gime and had landed a job at FSU, but only as a piano teacher. Several of us students went to the dean to see if it might be possible to form a chamber orchestra to be conducted by Dohnányi during a time that would not interfere with any regularly scheduled classes. The dean said the school of music already had a conductor (who was so memorable that I can't recall his name), and to have Dohnányi involved with the orchestra program would greatly upset the status quo. A few of us went to see the maestro to ask if he would be willing to conduct such a group if *we* arranged the details. He agreed, and things went rather smoothly.

But there was one rehearsal when one of his students was performing a Mozart piano concerto with us. The principal bassoon and the second oboe were both ill and therefore absent that day. I remain astonished and awed by what happened. Dohnányi told us to play without a conductor for the first and third (rapid) movements, then he went—without a score—to a small upright piano in a corner of the room and with two fingers played those bassoon and oboe parts. The incident became another legend in his remarkable life that made the musical rounds far from Tallahassee. He died four years later.

One of my best friends at FSU was Fred Hollis, and he was also a good tuba player. We had met at Brevard and decided to be off-campus roommates in Tallahassee. Fred was from nearby Pelham, Georgia, a village of about a thousand inhabitants, where his uncle was the chief of police. By April of each year this uncle was able to leave his job and spend the rest of the year fishing because of the money he raised from ticketing one driver after another who didn't slow down going through the town. Fred's other uncle owned the town bank and most of the city's acreage. For Thanksgiving 1956 Fred invited me to his parents' house for a very special dinner. What he didn't warn me about was his grandmother. Toward the end of a great meal she mentioned that she had heard that a local woman had married a "Jap." When Fred questioned her about why that was of concern she replied, "Well, I guess it don't make no mind, them Japs and Jews are all the same." The Hollis family was chagrined and I was outraged. But they quickly changed the topic and we all toasted the Pilgrims—whose attitude had not been much different from hers.

Later that year word went out that there was to be a "panty raid" at a female dormitory. Fred decided we should go but remain on the fringe, far from the center of the crowd. Everyone was enjoying the excitement until some do-good university official warned the males *and* females that this had to stop—now! When that didn't produce results he called in his reinforcements—about ten players from the football team. They stood in the front door of the dorm and challenged the group, "If you want to get inside you'll have to go through us." Challenge accepted, charge made, and the men went through and over the football players. However, that brought the local police and tear gas. It was my only experience with that stuff. We were so blinded that it took Fred and me about two hours to find each other.

Because FSU was a land-grant school it was mandatory for all freshmen to participate and pass a course in the Reserve Officers' Training Corps, better known as ROTC. Knowing that I would be transferring to Northwestern at the end of that year, I had a hard time taking it seriously. Actually, it would have been difficult to take ROTC seriously under any conditions, which is why I stopped going to class after the first semester. It didn't take long for an official letter to arrive stating that I couldn't graduate without passing this course. About a week later I received another letter requesting my presence—"Uncle Sam Wants You!"—for a meeting with the director of the program. That request I honored, primarily because I wanted to hear what he would say to persuade me to return to the classroom, and also because the last thing I wanted was another session with the dean of the school of music. What I heard was much about God, Country, and the Eternal Fight against Communism. However, his last line was the best. "When I was at West Point the class I hated the most was Music Appreciation, but I took it because it was required and I was a proper student. Think about that." When I thought about that I was never certain of his rationale. I did take the multiple choice final exam without the advantage of reading it and finished in about three minutes, to the utter astonishment of everyone.

ROTC is the only course I ever failed. My run-ins with certain authority figures have convinced me that many public school principals, coaches, and directors of ROTC programs are practically interchangeable. During the Vietnam conflict my only brother, Morty, phoned me to say that he and two of his high school friends wanted to stage a peaceful demonstration. I told him to get a police permit and gave him other advice. They followed all the instructions, planned their picket for lunch hour, when there were no classes scheduled, and planted themselves on a street across from their high school so as not to be on school property. However, by that time Junior ROTC had invaded public schools, and a few of its members got wind of this mighty protest. It took only a few hours for them to plan the terms of engagement, which included throwing large stones at the protesters. I always wondered where and why large stones were stored in a public school on that day. The result was that the principal, a former football coach, suspended my brother and his friends for one week for "Disturbing Campus Tranquility." And when Morty's student status was reinstated the principal said to him, "You should be more like your older brother, who was a model student and is indeed an outstanding American citizen." Morty decided it wouldn't help his cause if he told the principal that his "outstanding citizen" older brother was participating almost daily in antiwar marches in New York City and had hair that fell below his shoulders.

In 1957, when I entered Northwestern, my family was decidedly middle-class. My father was by then a traveling salesman. He worked hard (he was out the door early each Monday and generally returned late the following Friday), but he never believed in the words of Joe E. Lewis: "A friend in need is a pest." He was a sucker for anybody who needed a loan. When he had a heart attack at age seventy-two, my brother and I went to his office to look at the official papers in his safe. Mostly what we found were IOU's from numerous "friends," a number of whom had already died. My father eventually did quite well financially but, as a good family friend once said, despite himself.

I arrived at Evanston four days before registration, quickly found an apartment, and unpacked. First thing the next morning I headed over to the music school to find a practice room. I had just finished my warm-up routine and was preparing to do some work on the Brahms Horn Trio when I heard another horn player several rooms away. He was doing things on the instrument I hadn't thought possible, and I was so overwhelmed by his ability that I wondered at that moment if I should just repack and go home. If what I heard was typical of students in Phil Farkas's studio, I had no business being there. I worried as I played through the first movement of the Brahms and was startled when I heard a knock on my door. Looking up, I saw a friendly face, and I motioned for him to enter. What Dave Krehbiel said was: "You sound pretty good, nice deep tone. Sorry to interrupt, but I wondered if you might want to go across the street for a cup of coffee." Within a few minutes I found out that Dave

17

had just been named assistant principal horn in the Chicago Symphony Orchestra and had decided to take a few courses toward his master's degree during their season. It certainly was a relief to know he wasn't the immediate competition. I didn't have to pack up.

I had my NU scholarship as promised, but room and board were not covered, so I got a job with an already infamous, just-off-campus eatery called The Hut. The Hut was essentially a coffeehouse hangout for students from the NU music and theater schools. What I learned in the three years I worked there is not in any book. My duties were waiting on tables, cooking (although hot meals that appeared on the menu were seldom available), making sandwiches, and washing dishes. The owner was too cheap to purchase an automatic dishwasher. I can't imagine there are too many people who have washed as many dishes in a lifetime as I did in my three years at The Hut. The owner was Irv, a kind and honorable person. Irv had even hired his detested brother-in-law, Hank, as a partner of sorts. Hank was seldom seen, for which all the employees were grateful. He was the type of glad-hander who made all he encountered want to quickly check their wallets after the first handshake.

A mother of an NU student once came in, asked to see the menu, and ordered liver and onions. I went back to the kitchen, couldn't find any liver, and called Hank on the speakerphone. He said to look at the bottom of the freezer under the packed ice. Lo and behold: a piece of liver! Green and vile. When I showed it to Hank he said, "Just cook it well done in a lot of butter." I did it, but the customer could smell through the sauce and sent it back. Hank had the nerve to try to get her to pay for it anyway.

Irv paid me sixty cents per hour for the entire three years. He had an eagle eye and was quick to say to any student who came to the checkout counter to pay for two cups of coffee, "Don't try to bullshit me, you had four. Pay up." But Irv, beneath his gruff exterior, was a "mensch" revered by all the students. Years later, when my brother was trying to decide where to go to college, we stopped off in Evanston, walked into The Hut in mid-afternoon, and took a booth. Irv, whom I had not seen for eight years, walked over and said to my brother, "What can I get for you?" To me he said, "What the hell are you doing in here, you rotten son of a bitch?" Which meant: "Great to see you again; it's been much too long between visits."

One time when I went to work I found Irv really down in the dumps. When I asked him what the problem was, he told me that his Jewish daughter had told him and his wife the night before that she was going to marry a Baptist. Furthermore, he had decided to disinherit her. When I asked if that would be permanent he looked up and said, "Oh, no, probably at most two weeks."

It should be noted that in late 1960 the NU football team was doing quite well even while many in the academic community were suggesting that the university should pull out of the Big Ten Conference. When I was there the great national football power from the University of Oklahoma came to play. On the Saturday of the game about one-third of the Oklahoma players awoke with some type of food poisoning. Since those very players had eaten at The Hut the evening before, we were visited by members of the Chicago Board of Health. It was never proven beyond a reasonable doubt that The Hut wasn't the cause.

The people I met in The Hut ranged from Rudy, a great hustler who enjoyed slamming on his brakes in hopes that someone would hit him from behind and he could once again collect insurance money, to Curtis, the head cook and a jazz aficionado, to Richard Benjamin, who was then an NU drama student. I actually had a very minor role in a play — *The Visit*—he directed. It was a role so minor that nobody in the Theater School would accept it. I also met there a great roommate and lifelong friend, Michael McClory, whose father, the Honorable Robert McClory, was the first Republican member of Congress to break ranks during the House Judiciary Committee's impeachment hearings of President Nixon. In fact, Robert McClory wrote the third Article of Impeachment—a true act of courage for any politician. It cost McClory dearly: his own party forced an end to his twenty-two-year career in the House by having his district redrawn. Others who hung out at The Hut included Ann Margret, Karen Black, Paula Prentiss, and Larry Pressman.

Money was always a problem for me. I could never fault Irv for not giving me a raise, even in my senior year, when I asked for an increase to seventy cents per hour. Irv just looked at me and said, "I'll give you the raise if you'll stop sneaking out the back door with those mounds of hamburger patties and institution size jars of liverwurst when you think I'm not looking." I'll never forget my shock. I had been ripping him off but

19

never thought he knew. Perhaps describing him as having an eagle eye was to underestimate his vision.

The only time I did have extra funds were the numerous Sundays when Curtis would telephone early in the morning to tell me that he was hung over and ask if I could fill in for him (with fifty percent overtime pay) until he felt he could get out of bed. But my best memory of Curtis was one Saturday just before midnight when he told me that I was going with him and a few of his friends to some no-name city in Michigan.

We went to a small bar just across the Michigan border, and I was the only white guy there. The featured performer was the great B. B. King, then relatively unknown, whom I watched and heard. Curtis knew of my interest in jazz and blues and wanted me to share and better appreciate this culture. Two years later, when I walked onstage to perform Mozart and Brahms for my senior recital, I looked down and saw Curtis, dressed in coat and tie, sitting in the first row. That man had soul.

Curtis wasn't the only instructor in my early jazz education. The Hut had a classical- and jazz-only jukebox, and it was a hangout for Bob Cranshaw, an important Chicago jazz bass player who later moved to New York and still enjoys a highly successful career. Through Bob I was able to go to various Southside jazz clubs where non-blacks simply never ventured. I was fascinated by the great players I heard. The atmosphere at most of the clubs was loose, the programs were seldom set, and musicians were often there to jam, improvising without the restrictions that composers impose on classical musicians.

Even now the majority of the cassettes in my automobile are jazz, which friends find amazing. Anyone, musician or not, who hasn't made the effort to listen to recordings of John Coltrane has missed an opportunity to understand that a great artist does not by any means have to be someone who performs only in the classical idiom. Ellis Marsalis, who must be regarded in anyone's book as one of the few superior musician/educators in North America, says that Coltrane is the Beethoven of jazz. I agree. Just listen to his rendition of "My Favorite Things."

I knew at that time of the racial bigotry that existed in my family, but it took a particular incident for me to discover the extent of my father's prejudice. He and I had seldom discussed politics at home. All I knew was that he had once voted for a Democrat (Franklin D. Roosevelt's first term as president), but never again.

Bob Cranshaw was going to record a piece with a large jazz band and asked me to take the horn part. The session was to take place at Christmas break. I was excited when I called home to say how fortunate I was and how the extra money would certainly come in handy. My father was furious that I would even consider being in a room with "those people." He forbade me to do it. We argued but he was inflexible. Of course I did it anyway.

During my junior year at NU I drove to Cleveland during Easter break to visit with relatives and friends and discovered that bigotry ran on both sides of my family. My maternal grandfather, Otto, was an Englishman who moved to New York City and married my grandmother, Ruth. They then moved to Cleveland and opened a furniture store they named State City Furniture. The real ploy for State City was to sell—almost exclusively to blacks—on credit for one year. When the 365 days were up and anything less than full payment had been made, Otto would hire thugs to go to the buyer's apartment and repossess the furniture, which he would then resell at what he advertised as great discounts. I know this because during that visit I went along on one repossession mission, and I had to look into the eyes of people who were begging that they had made all but the last payment or two. I saw the hurt and tears. I also saw the hate.

◈ I SOON LEARNED AT NORTHWESTERN THAT I NEEDED TO take advantage of all that Phil Farkas had to offer and as little as possible of what Thor Johnson thought he was offering. In addition to being a fine horn teacher, Farkas was a good and gentle man. Like Bob Elworthy (who was a former student of Phil's), he encouraged me to know the conductor's score, not simply to know how my part fit in, but to deepen my personal enjoyment of music-making. Perhaps the three most important things I learned from Phil were phrasing, concentration, and the necessity of behaving honorably offstage as well as on.

At one lesson he was attempting to articulate a solo phrase in Stravinsky's *Firebird Suite* and had difficulty finding the correct words. His

suggestion to me was to buy a recording, any recording, by Frank Sinatra, whose singing would help me understand how to make the solo line
one complete phrase and how to phrase over the bar lines that separate
one measure from another. It worked beyond my wildest dreams and
I've been a Sinatra fan ever since.

One day Phil called to ask if I would mind taking the subway to Orchestra Hall for my lesson. He explained that he had just finished a tough
rehearsal and didn't want to drive out to the Evanston campus because
he had a performance that evening. On that concert was the same Wagner composition that had a few years previously started me on my journey to Northwestern. About twenty seconds into the horn solo comes a
loud climax on the top note of the instrument, a truly fearsome moment
for all horn players. At the end of that lesson Phil told me that musicians
can never be timid, that they should always think in positive terms.
They must always forget the inevitable wrong notes and concentrate on
what is still left to perform. Once a note is missed you can't grab it back.
Phil also said, "In the Wagner tonight you're going to hear either the
loudest high C or the biggest splat ever played in Orchestra Hall." That
evening I was hoping so much that my teacher would nail that dreadful
final note in the solo, but splat it was. However, in a softer solo that followed a few minutes later he was magnificent.

Shortly before my graduation I was making the audition rounds.
When I was engaged by the Atlanta Symphony I hurried back to Evanston and called Phil, telling him I really needed to see him as soon as
convenient. I was terribly excited when I entered his house, but he told
me to please have a seat because he had some good news for me. The
Quebec Symphony had a horn opening and had called him to see if he
had a good student for the position. They were willing to take someone
on Phil's recommendation. An audition wouldn't be necessary. In those
days that was how it sometimes worked. When he asked if I would be
interested I said, "Sure, Quebec is a better orchestra than Atlanta and the
pay a good bit higher." But when I told Phil that I had signed a contract
with Atlanta, Quebec went out the window. In no uncertain terms he
told me, "Breaking a contract is not how you begin a professional career."
It was a lesson I never forgot.

Thor Johnson's classes were boring from the beginning. I can teach a smart dog to move a baton correctly in two-four, three-four, or four-four time in about ten minutes. That was about the extent of Thor's offerings. Mostly what we heard were his own personal stories (we believed some of them) from his days as music director of the 7th Army Symphony and the Cincinnati Symphony. He also wasted time giving us Italian/German/French translations of instructions that we would find in our conducting scores. Of course, most of us already knew these words, or, if not, we could have learned them from foreign language dictionaries by spending about thirty minutes in the library.

Classical musicians worldwide learn and understand at an early age about fifty words in those languages. Nearly all pre-twentieth-century composers (Richard Wagner being a notable exception) used Italian words for instructions, such as *presto* (very fast), *allegro* (a bit fast), *adagio* (slow), *con moto* (with motion). During the twentieth century many German and French composers used their own languages for these words, also adding others that were more expressive and precise. Other composers (especially Copland, Stravinsky, and Bernstein) used a mixture of languages. I call these words "clues" and view grasping them and their intent as essential before proceeding to study any composition. This is the primary reason any conductor can rehearse without knowledge of the orchestra's native language.

Fred Prausnitz, with whom I later studied in graduate school, told me about an experience he had guest conducting in Turin. Between rehearsals he was desperately trying to learn a bit of Italian. After the concert one of the musicians was congratulating Fred and happened to mention that a colleague had told him that he had actually enjoyed the first several rehearsals the most—before Fred was able to speak *any* Italian other than the common international musical terms.

◙ I ONCE HAD AN APPOINTMENT WITH THOR JOHNSON IN his office to get his thoughts about bowings for the Shostakovich Symphony No. 5. When I arrived he was not there but his office door was open, so I went in. We had all wondered what he was doing at Northwestern after such a promising career up to that point. On his desk, on top of his Shostakovich score, I saw an answer: a form letter from the

Phoenix Symphony rejecting his application as music director. I regretted reading the letter and immediately left feeling both guilty and sad. Thor Johnson, my hero of only a few previous years, had still not realized that his glory days were a thing of the past.

Recently I received a letter from the great violinist Franco Gulli. What Franco wrote in part was that he was thinking of forgoing future public performances because he realized that he could not continue to play at the same level as he had in his younger years. It takes a person of very special insight and courage to recognize when it is time to stop. Larry Bird and Beverly Sills understood that. Muhammad Ali and Germany's former chancellor Helmut Kohl did not.

There were other disappointments for me at Northwestern. The professor of my Music Literature and Analysis class was almost as tedious as Thor Johnson. In addition to teaching, he wrote the program notes for the Chicago Symphony Orchestra concerts, which I suppose convinced the dean that he was a master of musical analysis. I received high marks from him although I often skipped the class, using the time for horn practice or score study. Although I always was certain to obtain all analysis assignments from classmates, my papers were seldom in on time.

At one point during my senior year this professor asked me to meet with him and the dean. The purpose of this session was to "suggest" that my papers had been turned in late because I was waiting for answers from papers already graded and returned to other students. Rather than express my outrage at this charge, I asked that I be given any assignment on the spot and that I would have it finished within twenty-four hours. It took until the following day to realize that while I was playing fair, the professor was not. The lesson he wanted to teach me was not the one I learned, either. The assignment was the second movement of the Beethoven Piano Concerto No. 4, which I worked on throughout the night. I was at a loss, unable to break down the various sections and put them into a musically analytical statement, and I had to tell this to the professor. His gleeful response was: "Of course you couldn't find the form. This is the first example of free-form style in classical music. I think it was a good lesson for you." What a jerk.

But in a sense it was a good lesson. As my studies continued I realized that Beethoven was a compositional radical. He experimented in various ways, which often were widely ridiculed during his lifetime. From Joseph Haydn through almost the first quarter of the twentieth century, composers wrote symphonies with four separate sections, each called a movement. For a solo concerto they wrote three movements. In a concerto the first movement was usually fast (sometimes with a slow introduction), the second movement generally slow, and the third movement fast. The second movement usually had a primary melody, followed by a different melody, and then ended with a variation of sorts of the first melody. We call it Song Form A-B-A.

In his Piano Concerto No. 4 Beethoven rebelled against all tradition and chose to ignore any sense of the norm: thus the free form. It was roundly attacked by critics and the general public. In most current music appreciation classes, which are generally poorly taught, the professor tells the students that Beethoven's Symphony No. 3 was the beginning of the so-called Romantic era of classical music, because it begins with two slashing loud chords and without any introduction. Nonsense. In his Symphony No. 1 he had already become a revolutionary when he used a key signature in the short introduction to the first movement different from the rest of the movement. In his Symphony No. 7, when going from the long introduction to the exposition, he gave the strings and winds the same note (E) to play fifty-four consecutive times. The note was the same but the rhythm varied, creating an almost unbearable tension. Beethoven also was the first composer to use *sforzando* (heavy attacks) in an almost hammerlike way when the music was loud, and no composer before Beethoven had ever written a *subito fortissimo* (immediately very loud) from a *forte* (loud) or a *subito pianissimo* (immediately very soft) from a *piano* (soft). Both effects are staggering to the listener. If you listen to his String Quartet No. 5 you'll hear dissonances unlike anything to come until at least a half century later. Beethoven was *the* great innovator in classical music.

I was disappointed to discover that at times the professors at Northwestern fell prey to the athletic department, just as some do at any university with a big athletic program and budget. I learned about it in a Shakespeare class with a fantastic teacher. I was in over my head in most nonmusical classes at Northwestern. In this class most of the other students were dealing with *Hamlet, Macbeth,* and *Othello* for the second or third time. It took me several weeks to even begin to understand the language of the Bard. The teacher was a visiting professor from Berkeley, and his unique manner in the classroom—acting out all the parts—was a real turn-on for me. I realized that Shakespeare's work could be as vital and alive as the music of Béla Bartók or John Coltrane.

At the first class I noticed the star from the football team sitting close by. We had met at The Hut on occasion, and we went out for coffee after the class. I never saw him in another Shakespeare class until the final examination tests were returned. He got an A−, and I got a B. I don't know how he got such a good grade. Perhaps he was a closet Shakespeare scholar.

The most interesting course I took at NU, musically or otherwise, was Constitutional Law in the United States, which was team-taught by two graduate assistants. The bent was certainly to the political left; it dealt with Supreme Court rationale for numerous decisions, and gaining some knowledge and insight into such documents as the Constitution and *The Federalist Papers* was intriguing. At the time I didn't realize the degree to which this class was politicizing me. What I found most interesting were federal and Supreme Court decisions that were increasingly protective of minority rights, often angering the Congress, the administration, and the public.

What I learned helped when I least expected it. My former roommate Michael McClory became engaged to Nancy Douglas, a niece of the fine Supreme Court Justice William Douglas. At their engagement party in Washington, D.C., I suddenly found myself in the center of a disagreement with Justice Douglas. He was arguing that man is basically good until proven otherwise. My view was the opposite, that man is instinctively evil and only through good deeds can he redeem himself. Things got a bit heated, a crowd gathered around, and, although I knew I was correct (when I was twenty-four I knew I was right about a lot of things), I decided it would be best to "let" Justice Douglas win the discussion. (A minor footnote: Nancy and Michael never did marry. My disagreement with Nancy's uncle played absolutely no role in that decision—at least that's what Michael tells me.)

The summer after graduation I stayed in Evanston to continue lessons with Phil Farkas. Because I was able to work at The Hut full time, it meant that I could begin in Atlanta with at least some money in the bank. A friend had arranged for me to live in a local funeral home rent-free in exchange for answering the phone calls from doctors three nights each week. The only thing I had to do was get the address of the deceased from the doctor, then wake up the hearse driver and tell him where to pick up the body. The apartment was well furnished and a sufficient distance from where the bodies were prepared for funerals; the silence gave me plenty of quiet practice and study time. I did have to enter through the back door and take the elevator, which would stop directly in front of the most recently prepared caskets—open and occupied. Believe it or not, I eventually got used to it. In fact, sometimes as we entered, my room-mate and I would place quarter bets on gender or age of what we were about to find. Only once did the arrangement cause a problem: the first time my mother telephoned. I had given her my number but had not told her what type of establishment it was, simply because it hadn't seemed important. The phone was answered as usual: "Hebblethwaite's Funeral Home. May I help you?" By the time the call got to me, my mother had moved from shock to fear to ice-cold anger.

During my last summer in Evanston some friends took me on my birthday to a concert at Ravinia, the summer home of the Chicago Symphony. The entire program (because of the length of the composition) was the Mahler Symphony No. 2, which features numerous solos for brass instruments. It was a wonderfully moving concert and afterward I ran backstage to congratulate Phil. In my search for him I saw the great trumpet player Bud Herseth and told him how much his playing had meant to me. His growled response was, "Yeah, what a big blow that one is." I was beginning to understand that even the finest orchestral musicians can lose their sense of inspiration after their three hundredth or so performance of a Brahms, Beethoven, Tchaikovsky, or Mahler symphony. And yet these works are all that keeps some of our North American professional orchestras alive—this is the music that sells tickets.

Tooting My Horn

Before the 1960–61 Atlanta symphony orchestra (ASO) season began, I went to an Atlanta music store to have a repair made on my horn. The owner of the store was Ken Stanton, which I (and many others) thought was a fake—a play on the real name of the nationally famous jazzer Stan Kenton. During a short discussion about my background, Ken said that he could secure a youth group conducting position for me in exchange for my promise to purchase only from him any instrument or other music needs. Ken's flagrant attempt at manipulation astounded me. A few days later a member of the ASO told me that this was the norm because music store owners in Atlanta were often asked to be the middlemen between teachers and public schools or youth orchestras. I accepted the position. The youngsters were for the most part not very advanced, and much of what we performed were arrangements of standard warhorses by the likes of Tchaikovsky, Dvořák, and Ravel. However, the spirit of the students was terrific, and for the first time I was able to begin conducting public concerts on a regular basis.

Because several members of the ASO had been on the faculty of the

Brevard Music Festival, I felt at ease and greatly looked forward to my first rehearsal in a fully professional orchestra. But I was not prepared for the idiosyncrasies of the music director, Henry Sopkin. Henry must be given virtually all the credit for bringing a minor league orchestra into the majors. The orchestra was able to perform free at the city concert hall because Henry had the foresight to often ply the mayor, William Hartsfield (for whom the Atlanta International Airport is now named), with bourbon at the Sopkin home. At one time he conned a car dealership into holding semiannual lotteries using the concert hall ticket numbers to determine the winners. He also took the orchestra on tours to every village within a sixty-mile radius. Our master contract stated that we received no additional pay or per diem reimbursement for any concerts within that sixty-mile radius, but we were paid for broadcasts when most of those towns began to air our concerts on their local radio stations. Henry was a master at hobnobbing with the financially and socially elite, a detestable requisite for music directors of all orchestras in North America. This paid high, though tragic, dividends to the ASO when a chartered flight from Atlanta to Europe for a tour of museums and opera houses crashed, leaving no survivors. Many aboard had remembered the ASO in their wills. Although the orchestra naturally had a board of directors, it was Henry who really ran the organization. He saw to it that the majority of the funds went into an endowment and that each musician received a bonus for performing a special concert in memory of those he had courted for years.

Although many questioned his musicianship and programming ideas (he once reversed the order of the third and fourth movements of the Tchaikovsky *Pathetic Symphony* because he thought the audience would prefer a loud and fast ending!), his dedication to the players was never in doubt. And he was very much in the forefront of engaging up-and-coming guest soloists.

Henry always tried to intimidate new ASO members. Our first concert of my first season included the Brahms Symphony No. 2, which features a short horn duet beginning in the second measure. As soon as the other horn player and I had finished playing, Henry stopped the orchestra and asked the concertmaster if he also would question our intonation in the passage. It was a fearful moment for me—had I already blown my career in less than ten seconds of my first professional rehearsal? However, the concertmaster (bless that man) said everything sounded fine to him. Throughout that season-opening rehearsal I saw the same thing happen to perhaps five or six other newcomers. I think that Henry really wanted us to believe from the beginning that he could, in fact, recognize what was in tune and what wasn't. After a few rehearsals, none of the newcomers believed in his ear any more than did the regulars.

My dealings with Henry were always good, and I felt that he treated me with respect. When my first season with the ASO was nearing its close I received a letter from the Indianapolis Symphony asking if I would accept a position with them for the following year at seventy-five dollars a week, ten dollars more than my weekly pay in Atlanta. I went directly to Henry's backstage dressing room at intermission of our last concert (outrageous timing, but I knew he was leaving town the next day) and showed him the letter; he promised me an increase to seventy dollars a week if I would return to the ASO for the following season. And he kept his word. I knew that he would and never even thought to ask for anything in writing. The ASO 1961–62 season was twenty-eight weeks. It now is fifty-two weeks and the person sitting in my old chair today is probably earning (including recording fees) ninety thousand dollars a year. But that was forty years ago and, in any event, I always had enough money on hand from the youth orchestra and the ASO to spend on girlfriends and to buy marijuana.

To put that orchestra pay in perspective: we used to buy the dope from a jazz drummer whose name was Spider Ridgeway, and it cost twenty-five dollars for a shopping bag load. Few people in Atlanta in those days knew marijuana existed, even most police. There were no secretive meetings. You simply called Spider, asked where he was playing that evening, paid the money, took the sack during a set break, and went home with a girlfriend to get stoned while watching Jack Paar—or perhaps it was Johnny Carson. When you smoke enough grass (I had learned to inhale by that time) it doesn't really matter.

I never understood the vehemence of the orchestra's attacks on Henry during my two-year tenure there. Yes, he was a buffoon in some ways, but a caring one. These attacks began on a low level but quickly escalated during my second season. Players would take turns playing wrong notes on purpose to test Henry's ear, and on tour the "pranks" went from lighting firecrackers in front of his hotel room late at night to actually throwing him in a motel swimming pool, which happened when a crowd was around him so that he couldn't know which musician had pushed him in.

I recall Henry once arriving at a rehearsal after having asked the personnel manager to place a glass of water beside the podium. When the first thing went wrong, Henry reached over to get the water, took some pills out of his pocket, and announced to all, "These are strong tranquilizers. Do you understand what you're doing to me?" And down his hatch went a bunch of pills. I always thought they were probably aspirin, but with Henry you never knew for certain.

When I told Henry I would be leaving the ASO after the 1961–62 season to start a music festival in North Carolina, he got tremendously excited about what I was planning and he offered many suggestions. I've never known whether it was the opportunity to replace me with a better horn player or his honest assessment of my ability to be a music director that fueled his enthusiasm. I would like to think it was the latter. In any event, we parted amicably and I sincerely wished him well. A few years later he was released from his position.

Toward the end of my first season in Atlanta I had heard that there was a horn faculty position open at the Brevard Music Festival. I wrote Jim Pfohl and asked about the possibility of his giving it to me. Pfohl wrote back that although I had one season of professional playing under my belt and had been teaching on a regular basis (that is what a good conductor does, regardless of the level of the orchestra), I probably didn't have the experience to be a "regular" (whatever that was supposed to mean) faculty member. What he offered me was a nonpaying job as a counselor and the chance to play in the same orchestra I had played in as a student several years previously. What I found most offensive was that Jim Pfohl thought I didn't realize that his offer was pretty much what I had received as a student, the only difference being that I now would be responsible for the security of teenagers rather than pitching rocks on a road. At that point I knew for certain how little Pfohl cared for others—whether they were students or professionals—unless he could somehow use them for his own benefit.

His attitude made me think long and hard about the possibility of a music festival that would exist primarily for the betterment of students. Rather than seeing the students as "cash cows" whose tuitions paid the salaries necessary to support the careers of others, I believed that they deserved to receive excellent teaching and the chance to interact seriously with the finest professional performers who were also dedicated educators. The Eastern Music Festival was about to be born.

Eastern Music Festival: The Dream

◈

DURING THE SPRING AND SUMMER OF 1961 I WAS INVOLVED in many long evening discussions, in both Atlanta and Greensboro, about the prospect of establishing a summer music festival that would focus primarily on student needs. Included in the talks were friends from my days at Brevard and regional music teachers whose students had been displeased with Brevard and Interlochen. The program at Interlochen was viewed as being a good artistic experience but compromised by its institutionalized vicious competition, pitting student against student on a weekly basis. Everyone who could be considered a founder of what was to become the Eastern Music Festival (EMF) felt strongly that neither Brevard nor Interlochen was an appropriate model for what we wanted to achieve.

Since I had originated the EMF concept and discussions, it seemed only fitting that I be elected to go to Dr. Clyde Milner, who was president of Guilford College, to inquire about use of the campus. Guilford is the oldest co-ed institution in the southern United States, a small but excellent college founded by the Society of Friends, more commonly known as Quakers. Clearly we needed a place to house and feed potential students, but what was most important to me about Guilford was that it had just received a sizeable grant from the Dana Foundation for the construction of an auditorium. I have a vivid memory of that visit with Clyde. He immediately viewed my idea as an opportunity for Guilford to make a significant artistic contribution to the region. In retrospect, I realize that he also understood that such a program would bring to his campus concertgoers who could be prospective donors to his school. His prophecy was correct—as I write, the board of trustees at Guilford includes the current EMF board president, one EMF board member, and the husband of one former EMF board member.

Clyde and I walked in the mud and rain to view the newly poured foundation for Dana Auditorium, which was initially intended for required chapel meetings and for theater productions. It turned out that Dana Auditorium was dreadful for both purposes, but it is one of the great acoustical concert halls in which I have performed. From a seat at the very back of the balcony you can clearly hear the softest note possible, whether the performance is by a full orchestra or a string trio—this in a hall that seats little more than a thousand people. No architect completely understands how to build a concert hall that will work well. The need for constant renovation of Avery Fisher Hall at Lincoln Center is a perfect example. It is mostly a guessing game. Nonetheless, for chamber music performances Dana Auditorium remains the finest hall of its size I know anywhere. Every member of the Guarneri String Quartet would agree.

During the summer and into the fall of 1961 my friends and I firmed our plans for the curriculum, selected faculty who we knew deeply cared about teaching as well as performing, printed a brochure, attempted to find mailing lists of potential students, sought free publicity, recruited students, and solicited donations.

The most difficult tasks were recruiting students and raising money for a completely new program. We made many hectic trips throughout the southeast to talk to students at junior and senior high schools and often to their parents at home. It was quite a challenge to persuade them to entrust their sons and daughters to an untested program that was being run by people not much older than the children themselves. We had to give many more scholarships than we had budgeted, but we had seventy-two students the first season.

Somehow it all came together because of the work and faith of so many. On the night of July 16, 1962, the evening of the first EMF concert, I feared the worst, wondering, "What if I give a concert and nobody comes?" I had scheduled a solo recital by our piano teacher, a Hungarian-American, Lily Keletti, who had taught at the Peabody Conservatory. I stood on the steps of Dana Auditorium and watched with wonder and pride as the crowd started pouring in. That opening concert earned Lily a five-minute standing ovation. The enthusiasm of the audience, soloists, faculty, and students continued throughout the season. All the concerts that followed—orchestral and chamber music—were equally successful in terms of fine performances and tickets sold.

The morning after the last concert I watched the tears run down the students' faces as they said good-bye to recently made friends with whom they had shared daily life and music-making at EMF. What I didn't know then was that this scene would be repeated at the end of every following season. And how difficult it would be for me to see the students leave, hoping so much they would return the following summer.

Most of those first-year students went on to build wonderful careers as performers and teachers. For example, Eliot Chapo from Miami became, at age twenty-six, the youngest concertmaster in the history of the New York Philharmonic. When he auditioned for that position he astounded Pierre Boulez, then the music director, with his sight-reading ability. After hearing him play flawlessly every obscure selection the audition committee could find, Boulez brought out his own off-the-wall and devilishly difficult compositions for Eliot to play. No problem. Eliot did not stay long as concertmaster in New York, in large measure because the older players resented his youth. He may be the only concertmaster of the New York Philharmonic to have quit the position. Eliot now is a soloist and chamber music performer and teaches at Florida State University.

We also had to bend over backward to accommodate one young student from a small city in Virginia. Ida Bieler is now a member of the Melos String Quartet, one of the finest such groups in Europe, and she teaches at the Robert Schumann Hochschule in Düsseldorf. Her parents had to be assured that we could properly prepare her kosher meals from the food they had flown down from Philadelphia. But Ida loved having the opportunity to eat nonkosher food for the first time and her roommate discovered that meals for conservative Jews could be a delight—especially the kosher steaks!

Eastern Music Festival was off and running despite the hundred and one unplanned obstacles we had to overcome. That first season was indeed a learning experience, especially for me. When all the teary-eyed students had departed and all the finances reckoned up, EMF owed Guilford College almost four thousand dollars, a hefty sum in those days. However, since there could be no turning back, I took no salary from EMF and asked for and received a personal loan from a cousin, Jud Kane, in Arizona. I also accepted an offer to be an assistant professor in Guilford College's minuscule music department beginning in September of that year.

From the beginning I was determined to have a racially integrated program, not easily done in the South in 1962. We had only one black student that first year. When I asked Charles Blue, an African American faculty member, why, he picked up a catalogue and suggested in a soft tone that we omit the request for a photograph with each application. A few years later during a board meeting one of the members asked me, "How many of *them* will be in the student body this summer?" I said I didn't understand what *them* meant. The board member haltingly repeated the question. I said I still didn't understand. He said that we could talk about it after the meeting. When I later approached him he said, "Oh, just forget it."

In 1963 the North Carolina Legislature, prodded by then-Governor Terry Sanford, allocated funds to establish the first state-sponsored, degree-awarding arts school in the United States. There was great fanfare about what was to be named the North Carolina School of the Arts (NCSA), to be located in Winston-Salem, just thirty miles west of Greensboro. In its initial years it was highly regarded, but now is generally recognized as, at best, a second-rate institution, especially the music school. When the doors first opened in 1965, numerous fine musicians and teachers were engaged; they commuted between their major orchestras in New York and other large cities to teach one day a week at the NCSA. However, that practice soon stopped, and many area musicians were named to the faculty. My view is that it is essentially impossible for a North American city to have a major school of music unless it is also home to a professional orchestra. An exception is Indiana University in Bloomington, where great teachers are engaged full time and paid salaries hefty enough to get them to leave their orchestra positions.

The first chancellor of the NCSA was Vittorio Giannini, who had been on the theory faculty of the Juilliard School. In 1965 and 1966 he had asked for and received permission from me to audition EMF students who might want to consider attending NCSA. He and I had several lunches together and I thought we were friends. One day in November 1966 I received a call from Vittorio inviting me to visit with him in his office at the end of the next working day. He began that meeting with a challenge: "I'm going to start a music festival on our campus and unless you can get your board to merge with us, under our auspices, we'll drive you out of business. EMF won't survive to see its sixth season because I'll get all the funding I need from the state." When I told him that I would take his offer back to the EMF board for their consideration but that I would not back the plan, Vittorio started screaming at me. "You can't win a fight with me, Shelly. I've got the backing of the legislature. The Eastern Music Festival will never have another season and you're being a fool." I simply got up and left, his voice trailing me down the hall.

My first stop afterward was at Bill Herring's house. Bill had been a friend when he was the manager of the Atlanta Symphony during my days there and was then engaged in administration at the NCSA. He told me that he had heard no discussion of any summer program at the NCSA and that when you got to know Vittorio well, you just accepted his temper tantrums. However, I had made Vittorio a promise, and I took the matter to the EMF board a few weeks later. Needless to say, they were completely opposed to leaving Guilford College and its beautifully wooded campus and to giving up their autonomy. The EMF board president said he would write a letter to Giannini stating our position. A few days later I received a copy of the letter. But Vittorio never read it. He was found dead of a heart attack in his room in New York City that same day.

FOUR

It's the Baton, Stupid

Between the 1963 and 1964 emf seasons I realized that my conducting abilities needed substantial improvement. I simply did not feel comfortable dealing with our faculty orchestra, the Eastern Philharmonic Orchestra (EPO), which was quickly becoming an ensemble of superior quality. By then I had married Rebecca Rountree. I realized that if I was to make sufficient progress, I would need a two-year leave from Guilford College in addition to some creative financing. As I gathered information I quickly learned that the New England Conservatory (NEC) in Boston had a two-year graduate program in which only four conducting students were accepted. More important, it had a weekly repertoire orchestra for the conducting students and a teacher, Frederik Prausnitz, with a marvelous reputation. This was essential, since no amount of teaching can substantially help a student to learn unless there is an orchestra available on a regular basis. After my audition I was offered and immediately accepted a full-tuition scholarship plus a small living stipend. Clearly, Rebecca and I would both have to work to make ends meet. I was fortunate to find a part-time job at WGBH, one of the finest classical radio stations in North America, and Rebecca chose to work for an accounting firm, even though she was a fine pianist and a genius at "realizing" orchestra scores—a talent more rare than perfect pitch. (Someone who "realizes" a conductor's score on the piano must be able simultaneously to read and to play up to twenty lines of music that represent the various instruments and which are often in different keys.)

We took a small apartment three blocks from NEC. Our upstairs neighbors were Abby Rockefeller, a cello student, and her boyfriend, John Semivan, who became my closest friend in Boston. As things turned out, because of them and their mentor (Lee Halprin, who chaired the Humanities Department at NEC and became Abby's husband a number of years later), my political views moved decidedly more to the left.

In September 1964 I experienced the Boston Celtics, Cambridge coffeehouse discussions about political issues, Frederik Prausnitz, the Boston Symphony Orchestra, George Zazofsky, and Cassius Clay, as Muhammad Ali was called in those days. Watching the Celtics play in the old Boston Garden was a real treat. Up to that time college basketball had been my main interest, but seeing in person such greats as Bob Cousey was a real thrill. The primary running back on the Boston Patriots football team was none other than my acquaintance from my Shakespeare class at Northwestern. I decided not to contact him because I didn't really want to know firsthand how he got such a good grade in that course.

The New England Conservatory was not in a fashionable area. It was surrounded by seedy bars and bad restaurants (with the exception of one Italian place next to Symphony Hall a few blocks away), and there was a boxing gym nearby. One day John Semivan told me that Clay was going to work out there in the afternoon—did I want to go? *Did I want to go?* We watched him float, sting, and toy with a few sparring partners and the audience simultaneously. But he was not a clown. It was obvious that he was fabulously gifted in quickness and ability to anticipate his opponent's moves. And although I was opposed to professional boxing (how sad to witness one man trying to pummel another to the point of unconsciousness; how sad to see Ali these days), watching him that afternoon was like witnessing a great pianist performing the *Emperor* Concerto—a true artist at work. What was quite surprising was his physical stature. I had thought of him as a small heavyweight, but when he finished his work that day he walked by me (I had an aisle seat) and I looked up and saw a large, smiling man. I wish now that I'd had the nerve to speak to him. When people play the game of "Whom would you most like to have over for a dinner party?" I choose Muhammad Ali, Clara Schumann (did she and Brahms ever *really* get it on?) and Jack Nicholson (who would have the nerve to ask her).

It took me a while to realize that Fred Prausnitz was an interesting character both on and off the podium. He was an excellent conductor and, largely depending on his mood, could be a fine teacher. He also was a good friend. Fred's career has been all over the map. He had been on the conducting staff at the Juilliard School before coming to NEC, and his background included numerous concerts with several major orchestras in the States and abroad. Yet Fred has always been his own worst enemy. He once told me that if your employer (board or conservatory president) seemed to feel that all was going well, it was time to "create" a problem, to make certain that everyone knew that you were still around. This attitude got him in trouble at NEC and forced him out of his next position as music director with the Syracuse Symphony Orchestra. He eventually obtained a teaching position at the Peabody Conservatory, where he did outstanding work for years.

Fred was an honest game player and was always up-front with me. Once I was upset with him because an assignment I wanted went to someone else, and I accused Fred of being unfair, claiming that I was easily his best student at the time. He replied that I wasn't. He was correct. Fred once gave me the J. S. Bach Suite No. 4 as an assignment. When I conducted it for him in my next lesson he demanded to know from whom I had learned the correct style of Bach. I had to admit that I had always assumed that, since Bach gave no indications of tempi or dynamics, one was relatively free in terms of interpretation. Wrong, said Fred; go to the library and read everything you can find about the performance style of Bach. I did, but became terribly confused in the process, since all the Bach authors disagree with one another. When I told this to Fred he said, "Correct, but think of all the new options you now have that you *can* defend." Lesson learned.

Fred is the author of one of the few excellent conducting books available, *Score and Podium,* in which he remarks: "It was one of my students who decided that I should write this book. Sheldon Morgenstern, founder/director of a national music festival, took matters in his own hands when he suggested the initial funding of such a project to the Rockefeller Foundation."* I appreciated the acknowledgment, but that isn't the way I remember it. My recollection is that Fred knew I was going to the Rockefeller Foundation on behalf of EMF and asked if I would also be willing to ask for assistance for a book he was thinking of writing.

Fred was the first musician to speak to me seriously about accepting the intent of the composer. A conductor should never slow down, speed up, ignore indications of very soft or very loud simply because "it sounds or feels better that way." Whenever my instincts led me to make changes during lessons or while conducting the repertory orchestra, Fred demanded that I give him my reasoning, and much more often than not, it was unacceptable.

He also taught me, by example, how to get an orchestra focused. Toward the end of my time at NEC I realized that Fred would sometimes start a rehearsal at some difficult section, seldom at the beginning of the piece. When I asked him about this he said his purpose was to force the orchestra members to concentrate from the very beginning of rehearsal. Another lesson learned. I have done it ever since.

Ruth McKay, the graduate school dean at NEC, was in her first year, having assumed that position after a long tenure teaching college English, a position that had contributed nothing to her musical knowledge, but perhaps much to her formal bearing. One of the first things that Fred Prausnitz told me was that I needed to learn as much as possible about string playing and to register for violin lessons. On the following Monday morning Dean McKay looked at the violin faculty roster and said that she had met George Zazofsky at a faculty meeting and that he seemed like a nice person, and she assigned me to him for a lesson two days later. On Wednesday morning I went to the library, rented a junky violin for a dollar a month, and trotted off for my initial lesson. I knocked on Zazofsky's door, heard a "grumph," and entered. George was sitting on the other side of the room and, without looking up as he was writing in his

---

*Frederik Prausnitz, *Score and Podium* (New York: W. W. Norton, 1983), ix.

schedule book, told me to take the violin out of the case and play something. I was almost speechless (a first for me) and mumbled something, to which he responded, "Just play some scales, for God's sake." When I told him I didn't even know how to tune the instrument he became outraged and told me to come with him to the dean's office, where he told her in *very* strong terms that he was the assistant concertmaster of the Boston Symphony Orchestra (BSO), he didn't teach beginners, and she could take her assignment ideas and . . .

After slamming her office door, George calmed down and we spoke a bit about young conductors in North America and the obstacles they face. He agreed with Fred that every conductor should know something about how string instruments work, and he essentially designed a special course for me. Every week we would spend most of the lesson on bowings and how they affect every phrase. We worked from BSO parts, which means in many of my scores I now have bowings from Joseph Silverstein, who was then its great concertmaster. I did manage to learn to play a little on the violin, in fact enough that often when I guest conduct most of the musicians think my primary instrument is the violin.

Watching George maneuver in the politics of the arts was an eye-opening experience. He was in the vanguard of those forcing the U.S. Congress at least to listen to (with the hope of their understanding) what really needed to be done by the infant National Endowment for the Arts (NEA). His testimony before various congressional committees, printed in the *Congressional Record,* furnished me with materials that I used for nearly thirty years in my EMF Art & Society class. George later became quite disillusioned with the NEA, as did I. However, in 1964 and 1965 we were all giddy about even the small successes we saw in the radicalization of the way "people of power" were looking at all professional performing arts disciplines.

At that time the American Federation of Musicians union existed primarily to assist cocktail pianists and dance bands. George became a founding force in establishing a union more responsive to the needs of classical musicians, the International Congress of Symphony and Opera Musicians (ICSOM). Within a few years no board wanted to have to negotiate master agreements with ICSOM lawyers, and no orchestra member would agree to negotiate without them. As things turned out, the short-term victories of ICSOM often led to long-term problems, such as forcing boards and orchestra managements to accept financial agreements that could not possibly be realized. Today ICSOM lawyers too often mislead the very musicians they are representing, and too many board members accept conditions for long-term master contracts, knowing that when push comes to shove they probably will have rotated off the board, removing any responsibility for fixing the inevitable deficits that have completely shut down some orchestras. Despite the fact that the present outlook for professional performing arts organizations in North America grows more dismal with each passing day, all professional performing classical musicians now employed owe a great debt to George Zazofsky.

Many of the members of the BSO were on the NEC faculty, and I was fortunate to get to know most of them. Tickets for its concerts were generally available for NEC students, and the concerts were always exciting. All of us were eager to see the critique the next day in the *Boston Globe* by its chief critic, Michael Steinberg, who was a very knowledgeable musician. During my years at NEC he critiqued Erich Leinsdorf, the BSO music director, with great scrutiny, and the reviews were often not good. Nor were the orchestra musicians pleased with Leinsdorf. When his employment was terminated he quipped, "The only medal music directors can look forward to from their board of directors is the Order of the Purple Behind." Three years earlier he had been selected by *Musical America* as Musician of the Year. Leinsdorf was not exciting musically but he gave precise and literal performances. He has been unfairly looked down upon by many orchestral musicians for much of his career. There is a famous joke about him: when the manager of the Berlin Philharmonic shows up at the first rehearsal for an upcoming concert, he tells the orchestra that he has two items of good news: "Von Karajan is sick and Leinsdorf is not available as a replacement."

In my one meeting with Leinsdorf he told me it was essential to memorize and conduct without a score whenever possible, because you have but two means of communication with the orchestra, the baton and your eyes. I began doing what he suggested and continue to do so to this day, although it is tremendously difficult for me. I spend about forty to fifty study hours each time I conduct even something that I have performed dozens of times, such as the Beethoven Symphony No. 7, discovering new messages and ideas from the score while at the same time rememorizing it. It did not occur to me until years later that it was easy for Leinsdorf to give that advice—he had a photographic memory.

NEC professor Lee Halprin had a profound effect on my thoughts concerning art as it relates to cultures. He had left his teaching post at Harvard to become director of the Humanities Department at NEC two years before I enrolled there. Abby and her boyfriend, John (as bad a trombonist as Abby was a cellist), were already disciples of Lee, and they spent many hours telling me about his political and social views vis-à-vis the artistic life. Abby introduced me to Lee one day in a café. I happened to have just received the 1965 EMF student catalogue, and when Lee saw it he quickly read through it and, to my surprise, was quite excited with the program and the fact that I was founder and music director. What he really found astonishing was that I had already established the Art & Society class. I guess he was pleased to find others who not only shared his views but had put them into effect.

For the 1965–66 school year he had a similar course added to the NEC curriculum, and I immediately signed up. The assignments were demanding and the classroom discussions stimulating, in part because Lee was willing to pose serious questions that forced us to try to come to grips with ideas many of us had never before considered. Does art really reflect society or is it the other way around? Can art be made available to nonartists in a way that alters the direction of a society? Is art the means by which societies are eventually judged? The class started out with about fifteen students but later dwindled down to three. Most of the students either weren't interested in what was being discussed or didn't want to deal with the tough assignments. And that was a shame. Too few musicians are knowledgeable about anything other than their instruments, voices, or batons.

◙ WE HAD A CHILD! WE NAMED HER SARAH (AFTER HER POLish great-grandmother, Sali). By the time Sali (as we called her) joined us I had been given a secretary and the title of assistant conductor at NEC, which consisted largely of organizing and following through on undergraduate auditions. Often this was difficult because BSO faculty members seldom wanted to spend time listening to auditions. Though I was reluctant to do so, I often had to make the final determination.

After I had completed several sets of auditions I attended my first meeting as a member of the acceptance and scholarship committee. Also present were the undergraduate dean, the financial aid officer, and Dean McKay, who had seemed so prim and proper when she was assigning me violin lessons with George Zazofsky. I had prepared all the necessary papers for each person and was in the process of handing them out when, to my astonishment, she said that since it was going to be a long night we ought to get properly prepared. She whipped out four glasses from one drawer, a bottle of bourbon from another, and poured for each of us. And when that bottle was finished she brought out another! As best I can recall, about midnight we had far more than depleted the entire scholarship budget. The following afternoon I received a memo from her office stating that it would be necessary to have a second meeting to double-check the figures we had determined. But this time the meeting would be in the morning.

At NEC I felt that I was learning a great deal from Fred; even so, during the spring of 1966 I made arrangements through George Zazofsky to go twice a week to New York City to study with Gunther Schuller. I was a great fan of his and felt that both his demanding style as a conductor and his compositional direction were the wave of the future. Many musicians still get furious with him because he thinks he is *always* right—and he is! One of the most important things I learned from Gunther is that when something goes wrong in a rehearsal I should *never* immediately blame the orchestra, but rather look to myself. There is a very good chance that some motion I made was incorrect and caused the problem.

Only George, Gunther, and my family knew of these lessons, for fear that Prausnitz would flip were he to find out. Little did any of us then know that Gunther was soon to be named president of NEC and that, after a big blowup with him, Fred would leave the school in a huff. As Fred recently told me, "It was a battle between a son of a bitch and a bastard." Fortunately, the battle ended long ago and they are now good friends.

On a late spring day in Boston I had my final examination. Even now, close to thirty-five years later, my heart stops and my right hand trembles when I remember the scene. It wasn't that I was completely unaware of what to expect. After all, I'd been through a similar examination, or jury, for my Bachelor of Music degree at Northwestern University. I knew that my jury would be made up of faculty members who would judge my conducting and decide whether I would receive my degree. And I was very familiar with the orchestra I would rehearse for the jury: it was the NEC student orchestra, which I had conducted once a week for two years.

As for the repertoire, I had already conducted three of the five compositions that my teacher, Fred, had told me to prepare two months earlier. Of course, just because I knew the pieces didn't make them any less difficult to relearn. The three I had previously performed were the Brahms Third Symphony, the Shostakovich First Symphony, and Ravel's *La Valse*. New for me were Beethoven's *Leonore* Overture No. 3 and his Piano Concerto No. 2. Each selection has its own traps for any conductor, regardless of experience.

Brahms, just because of his orchestration and compositional style, is always difficult to play with clarity. It's very easy to make a mishmash of any of his compositions, unless you give hours of thought to structure and phrasing. The Shostakovich has devilish tempo changes, irregular rhythms, innumerable intonation problems, and technical difficulty for every section of the orchestra. The Beethoven piano concerto has many treacherous interplays between the soloist and conductor, places where either the conductor or the soloist can race ahead of the other. As for the *Leonore* Overture No. 3, it is fraught with pitfalls from the initial downbeat to the faster sections that follow. *La Valse* is a nightmare for every conductor and orchestra unless every nuance and detail are attended to.

I had prepared the pieces in the same way I still study for a performance. I read the scores, analyzed the architecture of the pieces, memorized, and heard the music in my mind's ear. What I had already come to realize is that studying a score, even having performed it before, is always a new learning experience. The serious conductor must continuously question his or her intentions and how well they were achieved during the previous performance. Also, I learned *never* to listen to recordings of the piece I am studying; doing so influences my interpretation and makes me merely imitative.

Although many of the NEC faculty were members of the Boston Symphony Orchestra, I wasn't terribly anxious or overly concerned about a few of them being on the jury. I knew I'd be asked to perform sections of three of the five selections during a forty-five-minute period. As I walked the four blocks from my apartment to the rehearsal room, I felt confident. In fact, I don't recall even having sweaty palms.

In those days NEC had the appearance of many European conservatories, somewhat austere from the outside but with a warm atmosphere inside and a lobby dominated by an enormous bust of Beethoven. I always felt comfortable when I entered, even on that special day. NEC's Jordan Hall, where my jury was to take place, is one of the great performance settings in the world. Its acoustics make it possible to have perfect balance within the orchestra, and you can sit beside the double bass section and hear exactly the same music as someone sitting six rows in front of the first violins.

I went directly to the backstage entrance; when I entered the hall, I was surprised by how closely together the curtains were pulled. In fact, as I stood in the wings I couldn't see any of the orchestra. At exactly 11:15 A.M. a stagehand opened the door, and I strode out to the podium, looked up, and thought about ending my career, not to mention my life, on the spot. There, behind the orchestra, was the longest table I had ever seen. And seated behind it was every principal player of the Boston Symphony Orchestra. I was terrified. That was my first and only bar-mitzvah. And I didn't even get a fountain pen.

The jury selected three of the five compositions and instructed me to rehearse a particular section in each of them for fifteen minutes. After about thirty seconds my initial anxiety wore off, as it does with any concert, and I went about my business as I normally would. The only upsetting moments were when I occasionally looked toward the back of the stage and saw some jury members furiously writing comments on their legal pads. That afternoon I was ecstatic when Fred told me that the judges were full of praise for my work and I had passed with flying colors.

After my last concert at NEC we left Boston and stopped off in New

York City to speak to an artist manager, Albert Kay, who had shown interest in me. There we were, the country bumpkins, actually finding a parking place for our Hertz rental truck. Rebecca took Sali into a small deli while I changed into a coat and tie in the bathroom for my meeting and the signing of a contract. Then, off we were to the 1966 EMF season, with a new degree in hand, a beautiful young daughter, and even a contract with an agent. Talk about being on top of the world!

FIVE

Local Boy Makes Good

JUST BEFORE GRADUATION IN 1966 I HAD RECEIVED A CALL
from Greensboro. There had been an amateur orchestra there for many
years but the board now had plans to begin paying the musicians.
Would I be willing to be a candidate for the music director position? Rebecca and I talked a great deal about it, our primary concern being that
if I was not selected it could be detrimental to EMF in the minds of
those area citizens who were interested in the arts. Also, we knew that a
Greensboro Symphony Orchestra (GSO) would never come close to
playing on the level of the Eastern Philharmonic, and I might well end
up being frustrated artistically during much of the year.

Nonetheless, in October of that year I guest conducted the orchestra.
The musicians seemed to enjoy working with me and liked my rehearsal
style, and the concert went extremely well. Six months later, in 1967, I
was offered the music director's position with a three-year contract, six
thousand dollars for six concerts annually. I had decided not to reclaim
my teaching position at Guilford College, and so I accepted the GSO
offer. I knew enough by then to tell the GSO board it would have to

work out the wording with my manager: I wanted to be absolutely certain there would be no interference in selection of musicians, soloists, or programming. This meant that my New York manager would take a 15 percent commission on my salary, but I would have peace of mind. Or so I thought. I still had a lot to learn.

I wrote a letter to the musicians stating that I would like for each of them to audition for me, but guaranteeing that if any of them did not they would not lose their positions in the GSO, although their seating might be changed. All I wanted to find out was where the strengths and weaknesses were so I could program in a sensible way. The principal clarinetist was a public school music teacher, and he complained to my former high school band conductor, Herbert Hazelman, who by then was also director of music for the Greensboro Public School System and who had been a friend and champion of my musical career. Herbert phoned and threatened that if I went ahead with my plan he would make absolutely certain that I would never conduct another GSO concert. As a result, about 50 percent of the orchestra members who worked in the public schools (about one-third of the orchestra) not only refused to audition but resigned from the orchestra. However, by that time I had become friends with many excellent area musicians and was able to entice players from the neighboring cities of Winston-Salem, Chapel Hill, and Durham to audition.

Thus, by circumstance rather than design, the GSO was immensely strengthened before my first season started. But the GSO board raised their ugly heads as soon as I set the 1967–68 season programs. I decided that the primary work on the opening concert would be the Shostakovich Symphony No. 5, a good test for the orchestra and a work I considered an audience pleaser.

The GSO Executive Committee called a special meeting with a clear agenda: to get me to change my programs before they went to the printer and get rid of the Shostakovich on the first concert and Bartók's Piano Concerto No. 3, scheduled for later that season. The manager of the GSO pointed out to the committee that my contract gave me and only me the right to program. Even though I prevailed, that didn't stop the arguments. At that session a longtime board member said, "While we're at it, is there any way we can keep the curtains closed until the orchestra members finish tuning on stage? The tuning really bothers my ears." She was serious.

I stayed with the GSO for five more years, and the orchestra accomplished far more than anyone had a right to expect. We tackled such pieces as Mahler's Symphony No. 6, Bruckner's 5th, Debussy's *La Mer*, Ravel's *La Valse*, Brahms's Symphony No. 4, Bartók's *Divertimento*, and other works of notable difficulty and came through with flying colors. However, my problems with the GSO board continued. Guest artist selection became an issue when, against my wishes, they engaged José Iturbi (who should have called it quits many years before) and Van Cliburn (who did call it quits just in time). Cliburn was the darling pianist of the world, tall and handsome, winner of the first Tchaikovsky Competition (in 1958) in Moscow, in what was one of the more outlandish examples of the politics of the Cold War. Most musicians then and now agree that Khrushchev was determined that the winner would be an American because he wanted to present to the world a false Soviet openness. Cliburn's recordings of the Tchaikovsky Piano Concerto No. 1 were breaking all classical music sales records. Since I had never heard him perform anything other than the Tchaikovsky and the Rachmaninoff Piano Concerto No. 3, I decided to see what he could do with something like the Beethoven *Emperor* Concerto. The answer was pretty much nothing.

Cliburn always traveled with his mother. When they arrived in Greensboro she was ill with a slight touch of the flu. When he and I did our prerehearsal work I realized that he had little concept of the piece or even of Beethoven's style. At the rehearsal (Mother stayed at the hotel for that) he missed an entrance, which was of little concern to me although it bothered him tremendously. After the rehearsal, as he was getting out of the car at the hotel, he turned and said, "When you come for lunch tomorrow please don't tell Mommy that I missed that entrance."

The board discovered that paying a huge fee to one superstar during a season didn't pay off, which was what I had warned them about. The organization was deep in the red on individual ticket sales that season.

The year before my second GSO three-year contract was up the excellent manager, Eve Hobgood, quit. The board chair at that time knew little about nonprofit arts organizations and much less about classical music, but his ignorance hadn't kept him from gaining the position. He actually believed that the arts should and could pay for themselves. That, of course, is possible if you can get two thousand people to pay perhaps a hundred dollars per ticket for *each* concert.

A very attractive woman came down from New York City to interview for Eve's position. She spent one day with the board president and he hired her on the spot. Her incompetence was as staggering as her lack of knowledge about classical music. She was late in depositing donations and filling ticket orders, and she had no bookkeeping skills whatsoever. But she did do whatever the board president told her.

For three years we had been sending out contracts to musicians about six months prior to each upcoming season. In addition to the salary was a reimbursement for gasoline for those who lived outside Greensboro. At approximately the time the new manager started her job, the board decided to eliminate the payment for gas—still another "penny wise, pound foolish" judgment. They instructed the new manager, who was just as clueless as they, to void the current contracts and to send new ones that did not include the gas reimbursement. The immediate and predictable result was that almost all the best musicians were insulted and resigned. The artistic standards dropped immediately.

It was time for me to leave, even though I had one year left on my contract. I was outraged by the board's roughshod treatment of the musicians and their disregard for legal, signed contracts, but I didn't want to stoop to their level in my resignation. I also didn't want to damage the EMF image in the community. So I agreed to conduct the opening and closing concerts and find guest conductors who would be candidates for the music director post. A dear friend, Peter Paul Fuchs, was my successor and for years after was engaged in many of the same arguments I had had with the board. Having fought the good fight against a board of mostly snooty socialites, I was actually relieved to be free to do more guest conducting and to devote more time to EMF.

What really bothered the board was the announcement of my upcoming divorce, which at that time was frowned upon. How could my beautiful wife and I do that to them? It would cause a scandal in the community and they would have to explain it. I was amazed by the number of female members—married and single—on the board and in the orchestra's guild (their female volunteer group) who telephoned me to say how sorry they were and would I like to come over for dinner (and whatever) such and such night when their husbands were to be out of town?

The GSO experience taught me a lot about how boards run (sometimes run into the ground) quasiprofessional North American orchestras; they put artistic concerns at the bottom of the ladder. That orchestra today, more than twenty-five years later, plays at a level several rungs below the level at which it performed when I was there. But they have money in the bank. In 1995 their music director quit in mid-season to enter a real estate venture in Florida, and David Parker, the board president, was quoted in the *Greensboro News and Record* as saying, "I would much rather have to deal with this [replacing the music director] than a major budget problem." This is the thinking of far too many board presidents throughout North America. The first issue is money, the second is art. The GSO has now become such a social instrument that parents who want their daughters to be eligible for the debutante ball must volunteer or donate funds to the orchestra.

◙ I DECIDED TO MAKE THINGS EASIER FOR ALL CONCERNED and moved the following year to New York City. I found an apartment on West Seventy-third Street in a musicians' rent-controlled building. The deal was that you paid a lower rent if you earned a majority of your income inside the apartment, for example by teaching piano or violin lessons. My good friend the pianist David Bar-Illan lived there and told me that the landlord knew nothing about music or musicians, and that he (David) listed his students as Horowitz, Rubinstein, and Serkin; he suggested that I list my students as Ormandy, Stokowski, and Szell. It worked like a charm, no questions asked.

What a time to begin a four-year stint in that city—1969: the year of the Jets, the Mets, and the Knicks, of working against the war, of wearing my hair down to my shoulders. Living in the city meant that I could take the bus to see my artist manager about once a week to bug him about getting me more guest conducting engagements. In turn, he continued to bug me about getting my hair cut. "And, please, the next time I send you to conduct an orchestra, don't wear a turtleneck and jeans at the concert."

Some time after my years in New York I filed for my personal dossier through the Freedom of Information Act, and after several attempts I received it. Everything was there. I was dumbfounded by which unimportant events were noted. For example, on an antiwar march with Bella Abzug I had a very short conversation with a man, who must have been an agent, who wanted to know why I allowed my hair to grow so long. I asked him why he liked his so short. On another march I saw a middle-aged women who was holding a "Nixon Forever" sign and was screaming at us. Said I, "How would you like it if you had a son who had been killed in Vietnam?" She said, "I did and I'm proud of it."

But those weren't the only subversive activities that made it into my files. I had also attended demonstrations at Central Park, which were easily broken up by New York's finest on horseback; I had gone to a lecture by Bill Kunstler in the small park near Wall Street where the police outnumbered the crowd; I had attended a session at the Brooklyn Academy to "Free Angela Davis" and even donated money afterward; and I had participated in the March on Washington. The best entry of all was my attendance at a huge demonstration at Columbia University. Jimmy Breslin, the columnist who was running for deputy mayor of the city, was the primary speaker. The speech went on until we began to hear a buzz from the rear, which soon turned into a roar. Someone had a radio. The Mets were coming from behind in game four of the World Series. The crowd dropped politics for baseball as the Mets won on that day.

Too Much Money, Power, and Pride

IN FEBRUARY 1968 I RECEIVED A CALL FROM BILL EVERHART, who was working in an upper-level position at the U.S. Department of the Interior. I have no idea how Bill got my name, but he told me that Congress had supplied funds to match a gift from Catherine Shouse to begin a national performing arts festival. It would take place on land that she had donated, Wolf Trap Farm, located just a few minutes outside Washington, D.C.

Bill asked if I would be willing to travel, at his cost (actually, the taxpayers' cost), to Washington to discuss the possibility of being the Consultant for Program Planning and Content for what would eventually become the Wolf Trap Farm Park for the Performing Arts. Catherine Shouse was the widow of Jouett Shouse, who had been a member of Congress for four years and had held several political appointments. She was also an heiress of the extraordinarily wealthy Filene family in Boston. In 1968 she was a member of the boards of the National Symphony Orchestra and the Kennedy Center for the Performing Arts. Her donation for this project included ninety-six acres of her Wolf Trap Farm plus $1.75 million. Although she was highly visible in artistic social circles nationally, she was unknown to me.

I agreed to meet with Bill, a man I liked immediately, who seemed to have genuinely good intentions to develop a strong program at Wolf Trap. I was offered a daily seventy-five-dollar consultant fee, not to exceed a total of three thousand dollars, plus twenty-five hundred dollars for travel and expenses. My assignment was to produce a report that would provide a model for an artistic program "For the People." Just up my alley. I accepted the offer on the spot. Back in Greensboro, I thought a great deal about the possibilities—a national park is one place where all strata of society can and do mix in a comfortable setting, perhaps one place where it might be possible to get across the message that art is for everyone.

I made a list of people I wanted to interview, set my travel plans according to their schedules, and decided that my first trip had to be to Wolf Trap itself. I phoned a friend, June Arey, who was then director of the Dance Division of the NEA, and asked if she would drive me there in exchange for a sumptuous lunch. June was super and drove me out to Wolf Trap, where, as I walked the grounds, my mind was going a zillion miles an hour—the prospects seemed unlimited. When we arrived back at her office there was a message for me from Mrs. Shouse, who somehow knew I was in town and asked that I be at her home for tea in thirty minutes. I felt I had no option. But I was curious about her and intrigued by the idea of a ride in a chauffeur-driven limousine.

The minute I arrived she demanded to know what my credentials were and how I could have been engaged without her specific approval, even though a bill had been passed specifically giving all development of the program to the Department of the Interior.* "Why, young man, do you possibly think you are capable of establishing a project of this scope?" Like many board members, she felt that because she had provided the gift, the criteria and planning belonged to her, layperson or not. In fact, without the knowledge of Interior, she told me, she had already engaged the architectural firm of MacFadyen & Knowles (which supposedly had

---

*Public Law 89-671, 89th Cong., S. 3423 (October 15, 1966), An Act to provide for the establishment of the Wolf Trap Farm Park, . . . sec. 2.

a specialty in the arts) to construct an auditorium that ultimately would bear her maiden name, the Filene Center. She also said that I did not by any means have her approval to continue, that she would phone the director at Interior and her friends in Congress to put a stop to my intrusion. I realized again the power that goes with money, although I had never before faced such haughtiness.

After twenty minutes of lecturing me and refusing to accept my involvement on any level, she pointed to my teacup and ordered, "Drink it." I said, "No," and pulled out my signed contract, which had no effect. She continued her diatribe and mentioned that she was planning to have a lengthy conversation with her dear friend Van Cliburn (even the highest of society love to toss names, especially of famous artists) about what the program should entail.

Hoping to head off any number of problems, I called the architects and was able to schedule a meeting for the following day. That evening I caught the shuttle to New York and arrived well-rested the next morning at the offices of MacFadyen & Knowles. The "meeting" was largely me listening to them tell me not only that they were architects but that they would be taking care of the program policy and I need not waste their time or mine. It took a good deal of arguing with them to give me a copy of their auditorium draft plans, which I discovered were dreadfully flawed. As I would later state in my report, they had forgotten such items as a stage lift and storage space for two grand pianos, necessities for any auditorium.

The following day I started my interviews, a process that lasted several weeks. Each person had received materials well in advance, to save time and to permit each of them to give me as much or as little advice as he or she desired. In the process I met with old friends (Sy Rosen, Gunther Schuller, Stephen Benedict, Bill Herring, and George Zazofsky) and made new acquaintances (August Heckscher, Harold Clurman, Leonard Bernstein, Bob Joffrey, and William Schuman). This is not by any means a complete list but it represents, with the exception of Bernstein, those who were most helpful and serious. I had known Steve Benedict in his position as director of the Rockefeller Brothers Fund, which had donated money to EMF for scholarships for students of color. Steve made many of the decisions for the Fund and was an innovator, getting the Fund to make donations to such organizations as the Southern Poverty Law Center when almost no one knew it existed. Sy Rosen was then executive director of the American Symphony Orchestra League (ASOL), a post he would soon leave for the Pittsburgh Symphony when he realized that the ASOL was an outdated organization.

Leonard Bernstein agreed to meet with me in his luxurious private studio after one of his New York Philharmonic rehearsals at Lincoln Center. I walked onstage and had a tremendous shock. This man was barely over five feet tall and I found myself looking *down* at an idol. The interview with him was the least productive of all. He knew Mrs. Shouse and seemed very hesitant to make any suggestions that could be even the slightest bit controversial. Even a man of his stature in the arts world understood who buttered the bread. I spent most of my time in that room trying to convince him that, no, we had never previously met. Just as I was getting up to leave he leaned over just inches from my face, looked deeply into my eyes, and said, "Are you absolutely certain?" When Bernstein died I found it surprising that the European press was so aware of his numerous sexual advances, especially toward young male conductors. His passing was not noted with much kindness outside North America.

William Schuman, a composer and at that time president of the Juilliard School, and August Heckscher, then director of the 20th Century Fund, were both helpful. Yet the two best interviewees were Harold Clurman and Bob Joffrey. I'll never forget Clurman's remark, "I just heard that Houston is planning to have a new professional repertory theater company, isn't that fantastic?" After about thirty seconds of silence he added, "Of course, Amsterdam has eleven." Bob Joffrey was far and away the best of the twenty-three people with whom I spoke. He gave me an entire day, although once in a while he would take me with him to one of his various studios to check out what was going on in rehearsals. There was a spirit about that man that was utterly contagious, and it infected his dancers, who gave him incredible amounts of overtime at no extra pay. He understood that he had a wonderful and devoted dance company, and he spoke a great deal of the days before the Joffrey Ballet was famous, of the days when they traveled on the cheapest buses available and danced to "canned" music. When we met he was in the enviable position of having to turn away possible designated donations because a particular area of need had already been funded.

Ideas for Wolf Trap flowed easily from him. He did take issue (always cordially) with some of my proposals, such as having only one resident orchestra. Joffrey told me that among his ongoing problems was the difficulty of dealing with composers and conductors who lived hundreds or thousands of miles away. He often had to request that a composer add or subtract a few measures to make the music danceable, or explain to a conductor the difficulty of dealing with complex rhythms in an orchestration that might cause him problems coordinating music and dance. His major proposal was to utilize the cabins on the Wolf Trap property for regular collaborations among composers, conductors, and choreographers for commissioned works. When Robert Joffrey died, North America lost one of its greatest creative artists.

For the next several months I divided my time between guest conducting, EMF and GSO planning, and finishing my Wolf Trap report. Included were not only the results of the interviews but also the programs of other national festivals (including EMF's) and my specific ideas for bringing great art and the masses together. I wanted to create a situation in which anyone could go to performances of ballet, chamber music, opera, orchestra, theater, and the rehearsals for each; attend and participate in informal lectures and seminars that included composers, conductors, directors, authors, and performers; and, in a visitor's exposition center, learn the basics of playing an instrument, painting a landscape, constructing a set, or conducting an orchestra. In addition, there was an educational component for young students, plus the idea for collaborations from Joffrey. My hope was that those who would participate as audience would discover that the artist is not a magician whose feats are incomprehensible and whose art is only for the wealthy patron and the bored intellectual. The Marriott Hotel chain was just beginning and I had contacted them about the possibility of building a large hotel in the area for the artists *and* the public. What a trip it would be for Joan and Joe Blatz to eat lunch with Aaron Copland.

On four occasions Everhart offered me a contract to become artistic director. It was tempting, but it later became a running joke between us. Starting with the second offer he said, "This is absolutely the last time

I'm going to ask." And a few weeks later he would utter the exact same words. However, I was not about to leave EMF, where there was still so much that needed to be accomplished. When I was finishing the final Wolf Trap draft I flew to Boston, where Lee Halprin had promised to assist in editing. Very late one evening Lee turned to me and said, "They'll never accept this." When I asked why, his response was, "It's too radical, too rational, and too logical." And he was correct.

The current Wolf Trap program is now a mishmash of tired and old ideas, when it could have been something really special. Could have been, that is, if someone at Interior had had the nerve to say "no" to Catherine Shouse and her politically powerful friends in Congress.

Should you find yourself in the Library of Congress with some spare time, you might want to look at my report. It is filed next to a translation of *Reindeer in Russia*, which was written by a Russian conservationist. In the long run, his article was probably far more useful for the times than was mine.

SEVEN

But the Beat Goes On

PERHAPS THE MOST IMPORTANT ASPECT OF EMF THROUGH the years has been its 2.5:1 student-faculty ratio, which, to the best of my knowledge, does not exist at any other teaching institution, regardless of the discipline being taught.

In addition to their private lessons and chamber music sessions, the students rehearsed and performed weekly programs of standard repertoire in one of the two student orchestras. To give every student optimal performance opportunity, we were careful never to overload in any instrumental area. I was not willing to have players of any instrument sitting around with nothing to play for a week just to get extra tuition dollars.

Early on I decided that these ensembles would be on the same performance level and the students would rotate between orchestras for each concert to eliminate needless competition. Later there would be time for them to discover the competition among professional musicians, especially in North America. This rotation concept also allowed them the opportunity to work with several conductors during the summer.

Soon we also had a full-size faculty orchestra, the Eastern Philharmonic Orchestra (EPO), which I as music director conducted, as did several guest conductors. I instituted a weekly faculty chamber music series as well. These performance requirements helped determine the selection of our faculty. Each member had to be a first-class teacher as well as a top-notch performer, an uncommon combination. The piano department was strong from the beginning and was fully integrated into the chamber music program. Theory class was mandatory for those who could not pass an initial basic examination. I didn't want to have any EMF alum who couldn't recognize basic harmonic structures.

By 1964 we had 175 students. We encouraged those with sufficient talent to try the professional route, and the majority of EMF alums have been successful as performers. Many of those who pursued other careers remain involved in music in some capacity, be it playing in evening chamber music sessions, performing in local community orchestras, or serving as volunteers for area arts organizations.

In 1964 we began offering annual commissions to such notables as Lukas Foss, Karel Husa, Gunther Schuller, Bob Selig, and the poet and playwright Tom Huey. For the 1970 Beethoven Bicentennial, Selig (a former classmate of mine at Northwestern and at that time a faculty member at the New England Conservatory of Music) wrote his Concerto for Rock Band and Symphony Orchestra, which I conducted. It was a wildly crazy venture; it was especially hard to find excellent jazzers who could also read intricate scores. After many calls, I got help from Miles Davis, who suggested several musicians with whom he had worked. The performance was so successful that some of the students actually danced in the aisles. Iconoclast that he was, Beethoven would have loved it.

The most challenging commission came in 1993, when I asked Schuller if he would accept a commission to write a rag suite for full symphony orchestra. Gunther is probably more knowledgeable about ragtime (and music in general) than any other contemporary musician, and he did accept, although not until he had given the project much thought. Ragtime music is largely misunderstood by the majority of even the most studious musicians. It is the one musical art form that can claim its roots in the United States, and the "rules" that were in force in its heyday were strict and demanding. When most people think of ragtime, Scott Joplin is the only name that comes to mind. He was a genius, but there were many other talented composers who crossed the bounds of race, sex, and nationality. The form also attracted the likes of Debussy and Stravinsky. It is a shame that the life span of ragtime was so short, eventually falling into the hands of hack Tin Pan Alley composers who turned it into an immensely less sophisticated sort of pop music. Attempting to perform great ragtime music is a lot like walking on eggshells. It must be played with great delicacy and utmost care. What Gunther accomplished with what he titled *And They All Played Ragtime* was brilliant.

I was relieved that because of his obligations as music director of the Tanglewood Festival he couldn't be at EMF for the premiere of his work. However, I did agree to send him a cassette of each rehearsal by an overnight delivery service; the next morning he would phone to tell me what I had done wrong. I dreaded those conversations, primarily because ragtime music was still relatively new to me despite the homework I had done. Gunther was the living expert on the topic and in each conversation he pointed out dozens of things with which he found fault. "Your tempo at letter B is much too fast, the dynamic level at three measures after G is twice what it should be," and on and on. As usual, he was correct.

The problem that I found in rehearsals was that it is nearly impossible for today's North American musicians to play *exactly* what is written in true ragtime style without inadvertently adding a sense of "swing." They have the same problem with the Bernstein Symphonic Dances from *West Side Story*, a work commonly performed in North America, usually badly. The premiere of the Schuller composition was not nearly as successful as a performance of it that I conducted the following year in Poland. Most of those musicians had never heard ragtime, and they did play exactly what was written.

In 1965 I decided that it was wasteful for EMF to engage soloists to fly in, play a rehearsal and a concert, and leave the following morning. So I instituted our Artist-in-Residence program. Beginning the following year, each soloist was required to play a concerto with the EPO, perform chamber music with members of our faculty, give two master classes, and mingle with the students in informal discussions. It seemed to me that it was important for our students to recognize that even the greatest soloist is a musician, not a magician, and has the same hopes and problems as others. In later years some artists, including Gary Karr, the great double bassist and educator, preferred to do their concerto with one of the student orchestras.

The first person I turned to for help in finding guest artists was my old Cleveland neighbor Leonard Rose, and dear Leonard took part in EMF for fifteen consecutive years (with one exception) until an untimely illness forced him to stop performing and teaching. There are other great cello soloists of our time who have greater technical ability, but none could produce as deep and wonderful a sound. I have never known a soloist on any instrument who was as dedicated to teaching. I know that Leonard was proud of the successes of such former students as Yo-Yo Ma, Lynn Harrell, and Matt Haimovitz, and he often enjoyed speaking of a particular period when every cellist in the Boston Symphony Orchestra had come from his studio.

From Leonard I learned many invaluable lessons. For example, he told me that whenever possible I should negotiate the fee directly with the guest artist, not with the artist's management. For an entire residence we paid Leonard one-fifth his normal single-concert fee. After some years his manager demanded that the fee structure be renegotiated. Leonard told me to have EMF sign for whatever figure his manager requested; he would simply donate his "raise" to the Festival.

It always seemed that Leonard was at the Festival during the hottest week of the season. Dana Auditorium was air-conditioned, except for the dressing room. In 1981 he and I were waiting to go on stage, sweating like crazy in our frocks—the "penguin suits" we wear when performing—when Leonard turned to me and said, "Tell the manager to get two window air conditioners for this room and send me the bill. I don't care how much they cost." The many soloists who came after him owe him a huge debt. I suggested that we put a little donor's plaque on each machine but was overruled—too tacky, I was told. Some day I may sneak back there with my homemade plaques. I don't think Leonard would have minded.

Leonard did more to help build EMF's reputation than any other artist, and his performances were singularly wonderful. I remember one occasion when we were performing the Saint-Saëns Concerto No. 1. Just before the segue into the final movement his long solo notes had me mesmerized to such a degree that I forgot to give the next downbeat— until I heard a rather loud whisper: "Shelly, Shelly, I'm running out of bow." And I'll never forget something he turned and said to me during a rehearsal of the Bloch *Schelomo*. When we arrived at one of the beautiful Hebraic folk motifs Leonard said, "Two thousand years of suffering in this melody."

When he wrote to me about his beginning battle with leukemia, he ended with, "What you have created at Eastern Music Festival is like a small part of heaven." I flew several times to New York City to visit him in the hospital, bantering a bit about everything from Beethoven to how *I* was now responsible for getting one of *his* favorite students (an EMF alum) out of what was certain to become a terrible relationship with a budding young conductor. And from time to time his treasured wife, Xania, would pop in—once with a bunch of helium balloons. Months later when I was in Connecticut for a concert I telephoned his hospital room after rehearsal and Xania answered the phone. She softly told me that it was not a good idea for me to take the train down to visit. He died the next day. The musical world lost a giant and I lost a loving and faithful friend.

The 1966 EMF season was special for several reasons, not the least of which was that I returned from NEC a far better conductor, and I think the EPO members felt more confident with me on the podium. The Artist-in-Residence program took off with such luminaries as Michael Rabin and Claude Frank. It flourished as I later brought in such musicians as David Bar-Illan, Phyllis Curtin, Dorothy DeLay, Misha Dichter, Leon Fleisher, Lillian Fuchs, Franco Gulli, Nobuko Imai, Eugene Istomin, Gary Karr, Jaime Laredo, Julian Lloyd-Weber, Yo-Yo Ma, Shlomo Mintz, Leonard Pennario, Robert Shaw, Don Shirley, Joseph Silverstein, Walter Trampler, and Veronica Tyler, along with several string quartets, including the Tokyo, the Vermeer, and the Guarneri. The Guarneri's first violinist and their violist, Arnold Steinhardt and Michael Tree, have returned numerous times. Before his death the incomparable Josef Gingold spent eight consecutive seasons at EMF.

They all came regardless of EMF's infamously reduced fees. All our contracts carried a "Fee Confidential" clause, something that managers seemed able to accept since they couldn't control my personal dealings with the soloists. In Gingold's case he always said to pay him whatever we could afford, that he had all the money he needed and was only interested in "giving back" through his teaching. In later years the low fees came back to haunt me: EMF soloists would ask me to guest conduct for some other orchestra at a fee that amounted to transportation and hotel expenses, and *maybe* five hundred to a thousand dollars.

While my New York neighbor David Bar-Illan was attaining the distinction of having performed with the New York Philharmonic more often than any other pianist, he came to EMF six times at a fraction of his usual fee. I'm sorry to say he no longer performs because he has taken up politics as his major career. David had the dubious distinction of serving as spokesman and adviser to former Israeli Prime Minister Benjamin Netanyahu. When I last attempted to call him in 1997 I got an intercept in English and Hebrew informing me that his number had been changed and the new number was unavailable. If I were David I would have done likewise. I feel certain he was on the "hit" list of Hamas or other extremist Palestinian organizations.

In 1964 we began a series of what are now called "outreach" programs, sending faculty chamber groups to teenage summer school sessions, prisons, and day care centers. Today nearly every arts organization in North America has a similar program. We dubbed ours Project:LISTEN, and it quickly became so popular that our students also became involved. The increasing demand for those performances eventually required that I establish similar programs on campus. With one exception, I have never believed that busing thousands to an auditorium to hear so-called Young Peoples' Concerts has ever produced more than a handful of concert-goers or musicians. The one exception was Leonard Bernstein, but his kind of charisma comes along about once each century. The EMF concept was to target specific, small groups of listeners who would hear our musicians several times each summer. We insisted that the adults in charge of our young audiences not be present at those concerts, because we didn't want the children to be inhibited if they had a mind to dance to the music, try out an instrument, or ask questions. And I was always certain that any string quartet we sent out included two males, to dismiss the myth that male string players are "sissies."

In 1964 I began teaching an EMF class that I called Art & Society. I soon discovered that the class worked best when it was limited to twelve students. I served as a provider of factual materials and acted as moderator, and only two rules were established: no raising of hands to speak—best just to jump in to keep the twice-weekly, hour-and-a-half dialogues lively; and no sitting in the same seat from class to class. In our early years our topics generally centered around one issue: why should EMF be so concerned with teaching Mozart and Brahms when the government was involved in killing thousands of people each day in what the students called a "racist war" in Vietnam? The students questioned how high-level government officials or multinational corporate executives could in good conscience advocate a continued massive war machine and still enjoy going to the opera.

Once I invited an African American professor from Duke University to be a guest for the Art & Society class. He agreed to come but only on his own terms: the topic would be racism and art, and he wanted to address the entire student body and all faculty. Also, he insisted on a question-and-answer period after his lecture. His primary message was that black youngsters had no business being involved in a honky art form that was not a part of their culture. After his presentation he was lambasted by our black faculty members, one of whom asked, "If classical music is so bad for our race why are you here?" He replied, "Because Mr. Morgenstern is paying me $250."

The Art & Society topics changed over the years. The students often asked insightful questions: for example, why weren't board members chosen as meticulously and with the same scrutiny as orchestra members? We considered why the wealthiest country in the world is not willing to subsidize to a great degree its artists and artistic organizations when even the poorest of the world's nations do so. They concluded that art is powerful and the better the art, the greater the power; could it be that people of power do, in fact, consciously fear art? How can a great nation allow an entire generation to attend public schools that offer little or no arts education, when study after study shows that students who play a musical instrument are better achievers in such disciplines as mathematics and science?*

The changes made in the EMF curriculum were essentially for practical reasons, and we were light years ahead of most institutions in constructing such a varied program. In the late 1970s and early 1980s I realized that numerous orchestras, especially regional ones, were including in their audition advertising some mention of chamber music experience as a requisite for applicants. Those were the years when North American orchestras were beginning to realize two things that EMF had known for nearly twenty years. Audiences were dwindling because of the lack of arts education in the schools, and outreach programs by string quartets, brass quintets, and woodwind quintets seemed the only way to bring classical music to our young and to kindle their interest in orchestral performance. Also, taking an orchestra on the road to play for thousands of public school children may look good on a grant proposal, but if the programs presented are poorly conceived and performed, more potential concertgoers may be lost than gained. Unfortunately, though, statistics often speak louder than excellence.

EMF started with a healthy chamber music program, but it had not received the same emphasis as the orchestral program. Heidi Castleman, who had been instrumental in the founding of Chamber Music America and who is one of the most sought-out viola teachers in the States (she now teaches at the Aspen Festival, Juilliard School, and Eastman), had enjoyed a long history with the Festival, as faculty member for a number of years and later as an artist-in-residence. She deeply believed in what we were doing and in 1983 agreed to fly to Greensboro to spend a weekend working with me to strengthen the chamber music program in ways that would not detract from orchestral playing and would, in fact, enhance the student piano department.

---

*See, for example, M. C. Vincent and M. Merrion, "The Musical Mind Considered: A New Frontier," *Design for Arts in Education* 92, 1 (September–October 1990): 11–18; and F. H. Rauscher and G. I. Shaw, "EEG Correlates of Enhanced Spatial Performance Following Exposure to Music," *Perceptual and Motor Skills* 82 (1996): 427–32.

Since that time the Festival has had a weekly student chamber music recital, as well as the weekly orchestra concerts and piano recitals. I was able to find time to coach chamber groups, something that I always enjoyed immensely. Chamber music is the great love of most musicians, especially string players and pianists, because, in addition to being able to simply play some of the magnificent repertoire at one's leisure, there is an opportunity for self-expression that doesn't exist in an orchestra. More important, the study of chamber music makes each member a better orchestral player by forcing him or her to listen much more closely to the other members of the group, a habit that carries over to orchestral playing. Also, chamber music is a favorite of amateur musicians who can get together after work and play into the wee hours of the morning. It is one of the great addictions in music.

In 1992, when Joe Gingold was in his early eighties, he told me that he wanted to play a Haydn quartet on our faculty chamber music series. I quickly assented and assigned some excellent and enthusiastic young teachers to be a part of the group. After they had rehearsed for a few days I asked one of the quartet members how things were going. He said, "Great. We play about five minutes of each hour and the other fifty-five we listen to Mr. Gingold tell us fascinating stories about his career." The performance was really an event. In the first movement Joe forgot a repeat and the group had to stop. At that point Joe stood up and told the audience, "I caused this problem. Don't blame any of these children. We shall now start again." His comments endeared him even more to our students and audience. To Joe, anyone under the age of forty was a "child," and I became a "boy" to him only when he toasted me at my fiftieth birthday celebration.

Once Joe told me of an ingenious idea that Georg Szell came up with when Joe was concertmaster of the Cleveland Orchestra. Before the initial rehearsal for any given concert Szell would have an extra rehearsal with *only* the principal strings so that concepts and bowings wouldn't take up invaluable full-orchestra rehearsal time. Joe said it was a revelation even for him. The first time they did this with Szell the music was the Sibelius Symphony No. 2, which Joe had played perhaps five hundred times. Using the small ensemble revealed what the violist, second violinist, and cellist were playing while the first violins had a melody or vice versa. He believed, and I agree, that this rehearsal method was one of the primary reasons the Cleveland Orchestra, which still has key players who were trained in the Szell days, sounds like a large chamber music ensemble, always playing with incredible precision.

(Of course, in today's world such rehearsals would be prohibitively expensive, since they would add an extra service beyond any master agreement between management and the musicians. Since each musician in the orchestra has the same number of services specified in the master contract, each would have to be paid regardless of whether he or she had a note to play.)

Leonard Rose, who was the principal cellist for the Cleveland Orchestra until 1943, told me that Szell had another rule: office hours for him to deal with *all* nonmusical issues were from 9 A.M. to 10 A.M. each Monday. This great conductor wanted every available minute to study, and somehow he got it.

◙ ONCE I HAD BEGUN THE ARTIST-IN-RESIDENCE PROGRAM at EMF, the master classes became enormously popular, attracting eager listeners among the public as well as our students and faculty—me included. Giving an informative, useful, and sensitive master class is an art unto itself, so my search for excellent performers as well as dedicated and exceptional teachers was very difficult. However, the classes given at the festival by Heidi Castleman, Misha Dichter, Phil Farkas, Leon Fleisher, Claude Frank, Joe Gingold, Daniel Grosgurin, Franco Gulli, Gary Karr, Jaime Laredo, Wynton Marsalis, Leonard Rose, Arnold Steinhardt, Michael Tree, and a host of others have become legendary far beyond the local community.

Watching Joe Gingold, at age eighty, demonstrate how to project a true *pianissimo* to the back of the hall was a thrill for everyone there, and hearing Michael Tree talk about how a violist need not be concerned about which left hand position to use was a real revelation.

Witnessing someone like Heidi Castleman in a master class setting is much like watching basketball coach Dean Smith analyze a botched play. She has the unique ability to spot in little more than a minute technical and musical problems in even the most gifted student and make comments that result in immediate improvement that anyone listening can hear.

Michael Steinberg, the very knowledgeable music critic who was then at the *Boston Globe*, came to write an article about the festival and agreed to a question-and-answer period. One of the students asked him a question that became the headline for his story: "Do you get paid more for a bad review than a good one?"

Of the thirty-two years of EMF master classes during my tenure there are several that stand out, and not only for musical reasons. One summer David Cramer, the associate principal flute in the Philadelphia Orchestra and a Festival alum, decided to have a short question-and-answer session at the end of his second master class. One student raised his hand and posed the following to David: "I think I want to be a professional flutist, but there are so many fine flutists, so few jobs, and I have so much homework that it's difficult for me to find enough time to practice. What do you think?" David's response was quick and to the point: "What I think is that you've just answered your own question."

Wind players in North America have enormous difficulty because of the fierce competition and the few possibilities of employment. Harvey Phillips, the great tuba player and teacher, once told me that in an average year our schools of music graduate approximately a hundred tuba players with so-called Applied Degrees, which does not certify them to teach in public schools. And Harvey knew of but two orchestral positions that *might* become open in the next four years. What happens to the other 398 players, given that each orchestra uses only one? David Cramer was kind to answer the flute student as he did.

Another master class that stands out for me was given by the Guarneri String Quartet, a group remarkable not only for its enormous success but also because its original members stayed together longer than any other quartet of international renown—more than thirty years. When they were planning to come to EMF for the second time I suggested to Michael Tree, their violist, that rather than give their scheduled second master class for student chamber ensembles they should rehearse the music they were to perform the following night, but wearing mikes so the students could hear them speak to each other. Michael thought it a super idea, and so it was arranged.

Everything went well for about the first five minutes. Then Arnold Steinhardt, first violinist, and David Soyer, cellist, started a fuss about a particular phrase. This mild disagreement quickly turned into what seemed to me a shouting match, and I cringed in my seat, thinking what a disservice to our students my plan had turned into. After a minute or so (to me it seemed an eternity) Michael intervened, somehow things got back to normal, and they continued with the rehearsal. When the class was over, the students gave them, much to my astonishment, a rousing round of applause. I rushed backstage to apologize to Michael for my idea and started to say something about the fight. Michael interrupted and said, "Oh, that—that was nothing. You should hear what goes on when there is a *real* battle during one of our rehearsals."

The best single master class lesson ever given at EMF was by Joe Gingold. For his first student at his first master class an enormously gifted violinist from France had been selected. This young person really had it all—a beautiful sound, excellent rhythm, and an extraordinary technique for one of any age. Unfortunately, the student was also arrogant, which came out in his playing, not an unusual circumstance since most musicians "play" their personalities. Joe picked up on the attitude almost immediately. When the student finished playing he looked over at this greatest of teachers for approval. What he got was a dialogue, informative and vitally important.

> JOE: "What would you like to be doing in five years?"
> STUDENT: "I'd like to be appearing as a soloist with the great orchestras of the world."
> JOE: "Ah, but surely you know that only perhaps a dozen or so violinists ever achieve such a goal in their lifetime. Might you be interested in being a member of a string quartet?"
> STUDENT: "Perhaps, but only if it were a really good one."
> JOE: "Yet there are even fewer opportunities as a member of a string quartet than as a soloist. How would you feel about playing in a good professional orchestra?"
> STUDENT: "Never. You have little or no possibility of expressing yourself in an orchestra."

JOE: "If you cannot love playing a Brahms symphony as a second violinist in the last stand of the back row as much as playing a Beethoven quartet or a Mozart concerto as a soloist I suggest you forget about music altogether. Next student please."

How important that conversation was for everyone there. As for the student, he is now concertmaster in a good regional orchestra and we have remained in close contact.

◙ IN 1966 THE EMF ADMISSIONS DIRECTOR TOLD ME OF A fifteen-year-old he had discovered who was a composer and conductor. He had already directed a ballet he had written, conducted his school orchestra on several occasions, and won the Baltimore Symphony Orchestra Conducting Competition, which carried with it public performances with that orchestra. Two summers earlier I had instituted a Sunday evening sight-reading orchestra so our students could hone these skills by trying to play music they had heard our faculty perform the night before. I agreed to allow this young conductor to attend EMF and work with me, and, assuming he was such an immense talent, to share the sight-reading orchestra time. That is how Carl Roskott appeared in my life. During his three years as an EMF student and twenty-one years as a member of the Festival's conducting faculty I am not certain which of us learned more from the other. Fred Prausnitz had told me long before that you cannot judge a multimovement symphony performance unless you hear it in its entirety. To do otherwise does not allow you to understand the conductor's intent. However, it was from Carl, during lesson discussions, that I first realized that every composition is in essence one huge phrase. We conductors must decide how to break it up into smaller phrases to fit into the whole, but our overall concept must be to see how the very first note connects to the very last note.

EMF alums are principals in many great orchestras of the world; Wynton Marsalis has deservedly won several Grammys and a Pulitzer Prize and is one of the outstanding music educators in North America; many of my former conducting students hold or have held either music directorships or staff conducting positions with such groups as the New

York Philharmonic, Houston Symphony, Budapest Opera, Chicago Symphony, National Chamber Orchestra, Dallas Symphony, Indianapolis Symphony, Denver Symphony, Detroit Symphony, Brown University Orchestra, and the Orchestre de Cité Universitaire in Paris. However, in my view Carl Roskott is the most innately gifted student ever to have attended EMF. He went on to win major awards at the New England Conservatory and the Tanglewood Music Festival. His compositions include three commissions from EMF. He is now, by choice, the music director of the Charlottesville and University Symphony Orchestra. At Carl's invitation, I once guest conducted that ensemble and found it to be close to the same level as many so-called major orchestras. Carl's work there has been astounding.

A book long awaited by musicians, especially fearful conductors, was published in 1997—*The Compleat Conductor*, by Gunther Schuller. Gunther had earlier written me that he intended to pull no punches and he was true to his word. It is an ingenious book and a must-read for every musician, conductor or not. The jacket notes state, "Indeed, in these pages he castigates many of this century's most venerated conductors for using the podium to indulge their own interpretive idiosyncrasies rather than devote themselves to reproducing the composer's stated and often painstakingly detailed intentions."* One of the many examples Gunther explores is the so-called choral section near the end of the Brahms Symphony No. I, a section almost any concertgoer would recognize and where nearly every conductor slows down, even though Brahms wrote no such instructions in the score. I have always kept the tempo steady in that passage and when Carl first heard me perform this work he ran backstage afterward and gave me a big hug. The next summer he borrowed my score to look at my markings and when he returned it, he had written in a meticulous manner (and thankfully in pencil) the following words under each note of the ten-note choral melody, "This is the place where eve-ry-one slows down." Under the succeeding note he wrote,

---

*Gunther Schuller, *The Compleat Conductor* (New York: Oxford University Press, 1997), jacket copy.

"Why?" I laughed, but for Carl it wasn't a joke; it was, rather, a state-ment of respect. I felt honored.

Since the Festival's first year we had held a competition for instrumen-talists who were judged on their performances of selected concerti. The winner was featured in a public concert. By 1967 this Concerto Compe-tition had become a problem for me, and I had my first real run-in with the faculty. In my view competitions for teenagers are not healthy, and being involved in them is not my idea of a good time. In its first years we had the winner of the Concerto Competition perform with the EPO on the final concert of the season. Eliot Chapo was the first winner, Geral-dine Walther (now principal violist of the San Francisco Symphony) won the second year, and through 1966 each winner was either a string or wind player. The piano faculty felt their students were being neglected, and they demanded that at least one piano student also be a winner.

It was reason enough to call a full faculty meeting, and I fared far less well than I expected. What came out of that session was an agreement that starting the following year we would devote one entire concert to Concerto Competition winners, with all the requisites that constitute a normal competition—full jury, first round, semi-finals, and finals, reg-ulations on the length of the solo, memorization of anything written more than fifty years ago. Today the Concerto Competition has become *the* most popular event of the season with audiences, a development I find quite sad.

What makes this event so intriguing to the public and what disturbs me is the wunderkind mentality of North American concertgoers. It's the same as the fascination of tennis fans with Martina Hingis, of golf fans with Tiger Woods. EMF advertises itself as noncompetitive, but this competition is a great attraction for many students, especially the foreign ones.

Two EMF violin students—one French, the other German—reacted to losing in opposite ways. I had decided that the competition winners would be determined by the third week of the EMF season so that the students could get this out of the way (win or lose) and continue with their normal studies. When the French girl was not chosen as a winner she packed her bags and returned the next day to Paris—the only time this reaction occurred. And her teacher accused me of "fixing" the competition! She went on to win the Menuhin and other competitions, but she couldn't handle the fact that nobody wins every time out.

When the German girl was told in 1994 that she had not even made it to the finals, we had a long talk and I convinced her that the Concerto Competition was not that important. She threw herself totally into the EMF offerings in an almost obsessive fashion. I was so proud of her that I gave her the first and only (to this date) Music Director's Special Award for Excellence in Performance and Attitude. We have stayed in close touch and, having completed graduate studies in London and Vienna, she is now studying at the Juilliard School.

As music and education director of EMF I always went to the Concerto Competition concert, but after 1968 I stopped any personal involvement in judging, leaving this to my assistant, the assigned faculty, and the two student orchestra conductors. Despite my feelings about the competition, we have had, in addition to Chapo and Walther, such fantastic winners as Bibi Black, the first female brass player (trumpet) ever engaged by the Philadelphia Orchestra; David Cramer, associate principal flute of the Philadelphia Orchestra; David Hardy, principal cellist with the National Symphony; Manuel Laureano, principal trumpet of the Minnesota Orchestra; Ricardo Morales, principal clarinetist with the Metropolitan Opera Orchestra; Chauncey Patterson, violist in the Miami String Quartet; Guillaume Sutre, first violin of the Ysaÿe Quartet in Paris; and such piano soloists as Randy Hodgkinson and Gustavo Romero, among many others who have made names for themselves in the classical music world.

There was one competition at EMF in 1967 that I found totally appropriate. Charlie Castleman, then EMF's main violin teacher and the concertmaster of the EPO, had decided that the students should have a creative diving competition. Carl Roskott got to the finals by swimming out to the dock in the Guilford College lake, forcing himself underwater and diving *upwards*. When it came time for the finals Carl was taking a nap and was a no-show. He later complained to the judges that he had been sleeping on purpose, that his dive for the finals consisted of his dreaming of diving from his dormitory room into the lake, which was about a half mile away. The judges didn't buy Carl's con. I think they had lost their sense of humor. Too few musicians can really take a joke.

In 1982 I realized that EMF had alums who had achieved very important positions as soloists, string quartet members, and principals in many of the great orchestras of the world and as highly recognized teachers at some of the finest music schools. So I instituted the Returning Alumni Program (RAP), which each season brought an alum to campus as an artist-in-residence. It became highly successful, primarily because the EMF students could mingle with and ask questions of people who had "been there," who had shared the very same experience, eating in the same cafeteria and sleeping in the same dormitory. And, in some cases, because the average tenure of EMF faculty is quite long, the returning alum had studied with the same people who were teaching the current students.

One day during the 1996 season I walked into the cafeteria and saw Jim Lambert, our RAP person that season, almost in tears. Most of the students had eaten and gone so I went over to Jim to see what was wrong. Jim, who is the associate principal double bassist with the Cincinnati Symphony, told me that he had decided to eat all his meals in the cafeteria that week and each time sit with a different group of students. And, as was usually the case, they were peppering him with questions regarding what schools he thought were the best, how he liked life in a fine major orchestra, and whether it wise for them to enter a career in music. Jim said that he was just thinking about being in that same room at lunch many years before, when he got up the nerve to sit at Leonard Rose's table for lunch one day. That conversation, he said, was one of the highlights of his life. He also told me that he doesn't to this day recall a word of what was said, but that is not what was important to him. What really mattered was that this great musician would take time to talk to him as an equal.

For me, the most memorable RAP soloists appeared in 1995, when I programmed the Mozart *Sinfonia Concertante* and decided to invite two alums. Guillaume Sutre and Geraldine Walther were the soloists, and the performance was so astounding that I, as conductor, felt I was just along for the ride. It was the first and only time I had seen a spontaneous and immediate standing ovation for that composition. They were really something together. Their musical ideas were identical, they knew the orchestral score in minute detail, the sound balance between them was perfect, and neither tried at any time to overshadow the other. It was pure magic. How amazing that two performers, perhaps twenty years apart in age, could return to EMF and so excite the students and general public! Their chamber music playing and master classes were as excellent as the Mozart. Of course, I could have invited Perlman and Zuckerman rather than Guillaume and Geraldine, but the cost would have been about ninety-six thousand dollars higher and I doubt the performance would have been as good.

◙ IN 1984 WE BEGAN THE INTERNATIONAL SCHOLARSHIP Program (ISP), which brought many foreign string students from such countries as Spain, France, Czech Republic, Germany, Switzerland, Poland, Romania, Austria, Hungary, Israel, Yugoslavia, Latvia, and Belgium. Auditions were usually held in Düsseldorf, Paris, and Geneva, and the demand to participate greatly increased throughout the years. Although the original sponsors dropped out, others were found over the years.

A few questioned the wisdom of such a program on the grounds that EMF was giving a paid package of tuition, round-trip air travel, and room and board to six to eight foreign students each year rather than distributing those funds to Americans. That criticism is easily answered. First, without the program we wouldn't have had the funds to give to anyone, foreign or otherwise. Second, foreigners would have had little interest in paying the out-of-sight tuitions unique to North America; most European university and conservatory students pay only a token or no tuition. Third, we would have lost the social, musical, and, in some cases, professional benefits of the program for all the students, the importance of which cannot be overemphasized.

I scheduled each ISP audition for twenty minutes, to allow time to hear how well the student played and also to conduct a personal interview. I wanted to have a feel that the winners would fit into the EMF program in a positive way. On several occasions I didn't accept the very best players because they were interested only in winning a concerto competition in the States or they seemed to have a haughty attitude. We made sure that each ISP recipient roomed with a North American student to promote discussions about cultural differences, be it food, politics, boyfriends and girlfriends, or education.

The program was a wonderful success, and students on both sides of the Atlantic benefited. In March 1998 I received a letter from an EMF alumnus from Kansas City. He told me that he had attended a program in Germany the previous summer and there were seven other former Festival students there. EMF was the only prior musical experience these students had in common, and they spoke long into the nights about how much the Festival had meant to them.

In late May of 1991, well after the ISP decisions had been made and all available funds earmarked, EMF's indispensable artistic administrator, Renée Ward, received a call from a United States government official in Yugoslavia who said he had two gifted students he desperately needed to get out of that country, which was being ravaged by war. They had no money but could we accept them anyway? Without missing a beat, the administrator, who is even more of a bleeding heart than I, said, "Of course." She and I pooled our money, and they arrived. One of those students, a cellist, is now finishing her undergraduate work in International Studies at Johns Hopkins University, where she has a 4.0 grade average and hopes to work in international relations. The other student is currently continuing his piano studies in Vienna.

Other ISP winners have gone on to highly regarded orchestra positions, are soloists, or play in important quartets. But the best part is that they stay in touch with me in a way that is quite different from that of their North American counterparts. I usually hear from the latter only when they need a letter of recommendation, but the foreign students send me CD recordings or concert programs with nicely written letters telling me how grateful they are for having had the EMF experience. I answer their letters first, regardless of what is sitting on my desk. Some come to visit from time to time. They know how easily a smiling young former student can capture my heart.

Two of the 1996 ISP winners, one from Belgrade and the other from Barcelona, were students at the Conservatoire de Musique de Genève. (I had moved to Geneva, Switzerland, in 1989 and married Patsy Gray in 1991.) In September 1996 I took them to lunch, during which they planned an American Thanksgiving fête for other ISP students from France, Switzerland, Spain, and Germany—to be held at my house! I loved the idea, invited a few adult friends, and ordered two twelve-pound turkeys, which I thought we'd be eating for weeks afterward. What I hadn't taken into account was a dozen healthy teenagers and their appetites, regardless of the country of origin.

Beginning in the 1980s I started piling one program after another on the festival faculty and students, each in an attempt to reach larger audiences and to provide EMF with additional income. It was not until 1994, when I began rehearsals with one of the student orchestras in the Shostakovich Symphony No. 12 (a work that requires timpani and five percussionists), that I realized something had gone askew. At the beginning of the first rehearsal I was missing all the percussionists and four wind players because they had been assigned to play some grandiose composition with the EPO that week, and the guest conductor had decided to change his rehearsal order without notifying me. This was understandable, because most of EMF's guest conductors deal only with the EPO and have no sense of the overall program. At the end of my rehearsal two string students told me they couldn't be there for the last half-hour of rehearsal the following day because they were members of a string quartet that was to play an important outreach recital (arranged by a board member) in a neighboring town. I had to tell them no, missing the last part of rehearsal was not allowed, and then I went to the director of outreach and told her to get a different quartet from the other student orchestra which was not rehearsing at the same time.

For my second rehearsal all but three of the percussionists plus three brass players were missing because they had been assigned to play the EPO Pops concert in High Point. When we began to rehearse another piece I discovered that the music publisher had used inconsistent nomenclatures as guide marks throughout the score. The wind players had rehearsal *letters* in their music while the rest of the orchestra had rehearsal *numbers*, and of course none of them matched at the same place, meaning that there was no possibility of even attempting to rehearse. The librarian could have helped but she was with the EPO in High Point.

For the third rehearsal we had a problem with stage lighting. The stage crew student assistant hadn't yet been told how to work the lighting board, and we (the orchestra members and I) had to spend thirty minutes moving all the chairs and music stands to the front of the stage so we could use the house lights. After that rehearsal I asked the librarian to collect all the parts from the wind students and have her staff insert rehearsal numbers in the music so that we would be literally working on the same page.

With Native American week in mind, I had invited Louis Ballard for a residency that year, and a gracious and gifted person he is. However, without checking with me (for which I couldn't fault him, as he didn't know our rehearsal schedule or order) Louis decided to have a rehearsal of his chamber work at the same time as my orchestral session, and there went more percussionists. By this time I still hadn't had all the orchestra together, which actually didn't happen until the dress rehearsal. Only the timpanist, Jason Marsalis (the youngest son of that remarkable family), had been at each rehearsal. Thank heavens for that, because when there was a somewhat complicated meter change during the performance, it was Jason who stayed with me and my baton. Together we helped the orchestra get back on track.

High Point Pops, Native American Week, and Project:LISTEN were important. They all brought EMF money and fine publicity, and seemed to me valuable experiences for students and audiences. But somewhere I had allowed my priorities to get out of whack. We needed to find some way to harmonize our need for money with our mission. The students were there to rehearse and perform. I'd been involved all my adult life in raising money, primarily for EMF. But first and foremost I was an educator. I was not alone in my feelings about this—many of our faculty shared my views. We were concerned about finances but we were afraid our educational program was suffering from all these extra programs. There wasn't enough time to teach properly, and the students were burning out. This began to affect our student retention.

Curriculum changes needed my attention, and the board needed to know my plans. So I told board members at their next meeting to be aware of the issues so there wouldn't be any surprises when they saw the following year's catalogue and EMF's other publications. Normally I would have asked if they had questions or suggestions about such issues. However, these were in-house artistic and educational issues that could be handled without extra meetings. Interesting programs that also are moneymakers are attractive to boards, but if they don't further the mission of the organization they won't solve financial problems and will likely cause serious damage to the product. When it comes to educating young people, shouldn't quality be the top priority?

◙ AT EMF MOST OF THE STUDENTS SIT IN THE BALCONY DURing concerts. One of my great memories is sitting with Joe Gingold on the first floor just in front of the balcony during a concert. When the last note had sounded there came a rush of bravos from above us. Joe turned to me and said in his smoker's gravely voice, "Ah, the students." Joe always understood.

EIGHT

Board Games

THE PRIMARY REASON FOR BOARD MEMBERSHIP IN AN ARTS organization in North America is to give or secure donations, to give or to get. Potential board members need to be told that up front. Sadly, that is frequently not the case. Nobody ever twisted a potential board member's arm and said it would be broken unless that person agreed to join the board. Being a board member is a serious commitment and should be taken as such, especially as we move into the new century. How nice it would be to see artistic boards spend less time meeting and meddling and more time fund-raising. If boards would spend the time they squander on meetings on fund-raising instead, many major financial crises could be avoided.

During the 1970s and 1980s EMF went through many changes, some that worked and some that almost bankrupted the festival. In 1977 one of the board members worked herself into an officer's position and persuaded the board to vote that EMF would never be complete without a choral program. I argued as strenuously as possible against it, pointing out that for our age group of fourteen to twenty years we simply could not recruit enough students to pay for the cost of the additional faculty required, that youngsters that age go through voice changes without notice, and that we already had experienced problems pulling together from the area's amateur choruses enough good voices for Beethoven's Symphony No. 9, Mahler's Symphony No. 2, and Bernstein's *Chichester Psalms*. But they argued that at some festivals *all* piano students are required to sing in the chorus to ensure enough sound. I had seen this miscasting at Brevard and knew how abusive and damaging it was. I won the battle about the piano students but decided not to fight further. Fred Prausnitz had told me long before that a music director shouldn't pull out his or her contract any more often than absolutely necessary. So, while only I had curriculum authority, I was willing for the Festival to lose the money if the loss would convince the board once and for all what a bad idea it was. The choral program did enter the curriculum and it lasted one year only. When that season opened the admissions department had somehow managed to recruit twelve voice students, nine of whom were on full scholarship. We lost more money than even I had predicted, and before the next season the person who had suggested the program resigned from the board. I thought that was a shame, because she had a great deal to offer in other areas.

Another not-so-bright idea. There were two occasions, about ten years apart, when EMF board members decided it might be a good idea to add a jazz program to the curriculum. Meetings were held and more time was wasted, despite the fact that I explained at the outset that the cost would be prohibitive. My best guess was that a jazz program would cost EMF about $125,000 to start up, and even if we could secure the money we were likely to face the same financial dilemma we'd experienced with the choral program. Among the expenses would be purchase of numerous instruments (saxophones, drum sets, electronic devices), music stands, and music, renting additional rehearsal and studio space from Guilford College, and salaries for an additional librarian and a minimum of eight more faculty members. I also pointed out something I had discussed with Ellis Marsalis: as difficult as it is to find a full-time symphony job, jazz positions are about ten times harder to find. The jazz clubs of old have died at a much more rapid pace than orchestras, and it simply is not true that a jazz program at the Festival would have attracted a younger audience. The youth of North America probably know and care less about jazz than they do about symphonic music and, for the most part, they (especially white youngsters) do not even know the legendary names in jazz. Even when I got Wynton Marsalis to bring his award-winning band to Greensboro for an off-season benefit, the festival was able to sell only slightly more than a thousand tickets.

I won: the jazz program didn't get off the ground, and EMF didn't waste a lot of money—just scores of hours in meetings. Could it have been that I actually had better financial sense than many board members who managed or owned highly successful businesses?

There was one program idea I came up with in 1988 that would have worked: a string quartet in residence at EMF and, during the regular school year, at Guilford College. In fact, I had even chosen the members, each of whom was a former Festival student, a faculty member, an excellent musician, knew the campus, and was acquainted with the other members. For EMF they would collectively be the coordinators of the chamber music program, give a weekly series of master classes, and travel to several nearby cities for concerts. For Guilford College the benefits would be significant. Built into the budget was a salary for a full-time manager who would book concerts for them nationwide during the year, spreading the college's name and providing it with an invaluable recruiting tool.

Guilford is a fine academic institution, and there are many good young string players who might wish to major in another discipline but would welcome an opportunity to work with such a group in a college credit course. Since the quartet members would receive decent regular salaries from EMF and the college (which would provide employee benefits), their fee for concerts could be minimal: essentially transportation, hotel, and meals. I felt sure that this arrangement would guarantee a substantial number of concerts on various chamber music series, which would quickly spread the name of what would be called the Guilford String Quartet.

The college president, Bill Rogers, and other officials believed in such a venture and so did the EMF board. But it didn't happen. Our mistake was in throwing all the financial-need eggs into one basket, a North Carolina foundation that directs the majority of its funds to the arts, including EMF. We had several meetings with the director of the foundation; they were followed by a meeting with those who could speak authoritatively for the Festival and the college. The EMF executive director, Walter Heid, for reasons that would become clear later (see chapter 13), opposed the program. When the foundation notified us that they had decided against funding the program, I felt a great sense of loss.

Although EMF is without doubt recognized as a first-class institution, it hurts me to think about those things that we could have accomplished if fund-raising (or lack of it) hadn't constantly taken so much time away from developing our artistic goals. In 1994 the EPO was invited for a six-concert European tour. "No money available," said too many on the board. I unsuccessfully argued that the expense should be considered an investment that would eventually make a handsome return. Because the EPO is on a par with Amsterdam's Royal Concertgebouw Orchestra and much better than Geneva's Orchestre de la Suisse Romande, touring them would have impressed many Europeans and alerted major recording companies to the EPO's quality. Recordings would have brought in royalties along with money from different foundations, corporations, and individuals that had not previously funded the Festival. Why were board members who had made their fortunes following that saying "You've got to spend money to make money" shocked when I suggested EMF should take that same advice?

◙ THE FESTIVAL IS FORTUNATE TO HAVE HAD SIX EXCELLENT board presidents during the thirty-six years of my tenure. As things go in North America, a professional arts organization that has twelve of thirty-six years led by fine board chairs should consider itself fortunate. Our guiding angels were Herman Cone, Jr., Ed Zane, Leah Tannenbaum (who served twice), Joe Bryan, Jr., Gerald Truesdale, and Sam LeBauer. The reason I mention these people is not to localize or isolate EMF, but rather to illustrate what superior board presidents can mean to any North American arts organization.

Even before he became EMF's second board president, Herman Cone, Jr., an amateur clarinetist and an officer of Cone Mills, was the first person who bought into my dream. His passion for EMF continues to this day. Before the festival gave its first concert or enrolled its first student, Herman donated money and persuaded others to do the same. Without his faith and leadership there would not have been an EMF.

In our enthusiasm for the program and efforts to get it started we had overlooked one legal detail. It was Herman's accountant who caught the mistake when he questioned the claim of a five-hundred-dollar tax deduction for a nonprofit organization that hadn't yet been incorporated.

(Herman had a cousin, Edward Cone, who was a composition teacher at Princeton, and we offered him a commission in 1974. His *Stanzas for Wind Quintet* was of the meandering avant-garde style that was so prevalent then, and performers as well as audience were turned off. I sat with Herman and his wife, Barbara, during the concert, and when the piece ended, Herman said to me, "Thanks for doing this for me, but by God that's a piece of garbage.")

An innovative board president can make a world of difference. Ed Zane, the chief financial officer of Burlington Industries, was nothing if not innovative when he served as EMF's board president in 1969. We had a deficit that year (about $7,500, which seemed dramatic to the board), but Ed told me not to worry because he had an idea he was certain would work. However, he warned the Festival manager that it would work only once; from now on financial planning would have to be done much more carefully. Ed called an emergency board meeting, feeling that by using the word "emergency" he would get full attendance. Once the members had convened he walked to the doors, locked them, turned to the board, and told them the doors would not be unlocked until they themselves that very night pledged money sufficient to eliminate the deficit. This challenge came from a man who was only a bit over five feet tall and who weighed at most 120 pounds soaking wet. There were threats of resignation, complaints of blackmail, and general chaos for the next several minutes. It was difficult for me not to laugh at the movers and shakers of the city (all a good bit older than I) acting like children; wealthy people crying about their cash flow problems or business difficulties. But Ed simply sat in silence until someone finally said that she would sign a pledge card and have her husband send in a check for five hundred dollars the next day. It took about thirty more minutes to get the full amount donated or pledged. And nobody resigned.

Leah Tannenbaum, who served twice as board chair, is the spiritual mother of the festival to this day. She cared for and nurtured the program almost as though it were a child, through good times and bad, when we were in trouble financially and when we weren't. She, personally, and her family foundation initially sponsored such programs as Project:LISTEN, and they provided the money for the construction of Sternberger Auditorium, which is EMF's second concert hall on the Guilford College Campus. Their consistent financial support has been invaluable.

Yet this is only one aspect of what she has given that has allowed EMF to reach its present position of recognized excellence. Leah has probably attended more concerts and sold more season tickets in the past forty years than all other board members combined, and in any given year she makes an effort to get to know more students than do almost any of our faculty. Leah Tannenbaum is the type of board member or president that we all long for—she is supportive of the music director and manager almost to a fault, never interfering. But she does interfere with people she sees at receptions, weddings, dinners, always asking (even yelling across a crowded room) her favorite question: "Have you bought your EMF season ticket yet?" She unabashedly harasses not only these people, but any delivery person, the man who takes care of her pool, and strangers she encounters at the grocery store. It is hard to turn down a less-than-five-foot-tall, eighty-something ball of fire.

Joe Bryan, Jr., once said to me that his late father told him early on of his responsibility to the community: "It has been good to us financially, and we have an obligation to give back in a manner that is socially beneficial." Joe learned his lesson well and demonstrates it personally and through his family's foundation. During one season Joe, who was beginning a two-year term as board president, fired the manager, and personally paid off the accumulated deficit of eighty thousand dollars so the new manager could start with a clean plate.

The only retreat I found beneficial in all my years with EMF and other arts organizations was one that Joe conducted in 1984. He then owned a home in the North Carolina golf community and vacation spot called Pinehurst, and he asked all the staff and me to spend three working days there. Working days they were, too. Joe had an agenda that he didn't share with us before we arrived, and no one knew quite what to expect. Joe is not a musician, but he is certainly quite knowledgeable about classical music and opera. He began the first session by asking me to explain the entire festival curriculum in lay terms so he would have a more complete understanding. For some reason I decided to begin with the theory department, discussing the need for our students to understand the fundamentals of their art. After about ten minutes I began to jump to chamber music but was stopped—Joe wanted an explanation of the difference between major and minor scales. All of us were floored that we had a board president who really did want to know about our musical training system. It took me almost two hours to complete my theory lesson.

Joe also had a unique way of involving the nonmusicians on the staff. He had the marketing director, the bookkeeper, the admissions director, the development director, and the new manager go through their particular areas of expertise in much the same manner. When the three days were over we were not only a stronger team than before but also had a much more comprehensive understanding of each other's role in the operation. So did Joe.

Dr. Gerald Truesdale found himself with a terrible crisis when he assumed the presidency in 1991. He faced a staff fraught with dissension and an executive director who was playing games with the books. Gerald had been guaranteed that we were in good financial shape, and he had exciting plans to enlarge the endowment and to increase EMF's presence, especially in the African American community (of which he was a leader), something I had been working on for years. He was forced through circumstance to give up a tremendous amount of his time just to keep the Festival alive and make arrangements for loans to cover the substantial debts that had been hidden for so long. However, even though his medical practice (and income) suffered, Gerald was able to establish some ongoing fund-raising events, especially for scholarships, that have benefited the Festival in a multitude of ways. In terms of calling in chips, I have never seen anyone do it as well, with the possible exception of his successor, Dr. Sam LeBauer.

The LeBauer family has been part of the EMF tradition since the founding. Sam's father and two brothers also served as board members, and all of the family have been decent amateur classical musicians and important leaders in the community.

One of his most important contributions was persuading many of the best community leaders in the area to join the board, changing its face and attracting several large annual donations. Sam also learned that neither people nor corporations will necessarily donate funds simply because you are their doctor or friend, and he was initially amazed when he was turned down.

Sam once asked me to go with him to meet a wealthy businessman for lunch and to draw up a specific and detailed proposal for the funding of the Festival's International Scholarship Program—about $25,000 at that time. I handed Sam's friend the proposal as the meal began and he put it in his coat pocket. After we had finished eating, Sam posed the question in a strong manner, and our guest responded by saying he wasn't interested in any particular program but he did give us a check for five thousand dollars. Sam, to my astonishment, was actually depressed until I made him realize that a gift of that size from someone who had never previously donated anything to EMF was a great coup.

◙ BOARDS OFTEN BLAME DEFICITS ON PROGRAMMING, AND, for reasons I've never understood, Bartók especially takes it on the chin. Perhaps it's because many conductors don't understand his wonderful gypsy melodies and their orchestras perform his works badly. The attitude toward many twentieth-century composers reminds me of an episode from the television series *Taxi*. Jim, the recovering druggie, has a sister who is a flute player in the Seattle Symphony, and she comes to visit him in New York City. We viewers are informed that Jim has also played that instrument. The day of her visit is a slow one for the taxi company, so Sis pulls out some music and she and Jim decide to play some Baroque duets. At this point little Louie, the manager, played by Danny DeVito, goes into his office, picks up the mike, and booms out over the loudspeaker, "I never thought I'd have to say this, but no Vivaldi in the garage." And no Bartók in the concert hall?

How boards deal with deficits, after the panic has subsided, is fairly standard. First, they hold meetings to bemoan the lack of money, sometimes at the home of a board member who could easily write a check for the fifty thousand dollars (or whatever the amount) and halt the hand-wringing. Then they make lists of potential donors and decisions about who should approach whom for how much. Finally, one or two members actually raise the money.

Some years when EMF had a deficit, which was more often than not the case, we found nontraditional means of overcoming the problem. The EMF board twice imposed a deadline for raising the money. Get the funds by a specified date or shut up shop. Once Joe Thayer, EMF's wonderful dean for more than a dozen years, was able to obtain a one-time gift of sixty-five thousand dollars from a mutual friend who demanded not only anonymity but a rewording of our by-laws regarding board responsibility. The most important change was that thereafter each board member would be required to donate or raise a minimum of five hundred dollars and purchase a season ticket. The money and conditions were accepted, but the by-laws were changed a few years later.

Nothing lasts forever, especially promises made by many North American board presidents and members, as the Cleveland Orchestra so painfully learned in 1967. During a year in which they were negotiating a new three-year master contract, the musicians wanted the board to include wording that would give the players a strong voice in selecting his successor should their music director, the great Georg Szell, die before the end of the new agreement period. It was certainly a reasonable request, since Szell was into his seventies.

The board president at that time was Frank Joseph, a wily lawyer who had attained his position not so much because of personal wealth but rather because he was on the boards of various foundations and had a large influence on where those groups donated funds. He told the orchestra committee members that they didn't need to muddy up a contract with such details; they had his personal word that he would seek their counsel on such a vital issue. And of course the committee members believed him.

Szell did die before the contract was up, and the board began holding secret meetings to select a new music director. After months went by with no communication from the board, the musicians decided to take matters into their own hands. They held their own private vote on five possible candidates, then took out a full-page advertisement in the *Plain Dealer* announcing the results. They hoped this would preempt whatever decision the board had reached. Their clear choice was a fabulous and relatively young talent, the Hungarian István Kertész, who received about 90 percent of the ballots. Other choices included the even younger Daniel Barenboim and Lorin Maazel; the latter eventually got the position despite receiving the fewest number of votes—two. The board was outraged when the battle became public. Cleveland natives take their world-class orchestra quite seriously. However, as usual, the board won, the musicians griped to no avail, and the band played on. Fortunately Maazel's tenure was relatively short because under his baton the orchestra experienced its only downhill slide in my memory.

◙ AS FOR THE FESTIVAL, ITS DEFICIT WAS SO LARGE IN 1971 that even I was prepared to throw in the towel and would have, but for Jim Newlin. Jim was then working in the Guilford College administration and was on the EMF board. He was well aware of the Festival's financial problems that season, and he asked if I would be willing to meet with him and nine Guilford College students. I told Jim that I had a Greensboro Symphony Orchestra rehearsal that evening. He said, "Fine, we'll be happy to start the meeting at 10 P.M." The group called themselves The Guilford Ten, and a militant bunch they were. They accused me of being a quitter who was willing to rob youngsters of the opportunity to have the unique EMF experience. It took about ten minutes for me to climb on their bandwagon. Guilford College had given them permission not only to miss some classes but also to use the college's telephone switchboard for several hours a day for one week. They went for broke. Two of them even went to Winston-Salem, getting Gordon Hanes (of Hanes Hosiery fame and a wealthy arts patron) to walk out of his Rotary Club meeting and write them a check for five thousand dollars.

When the EMF board next met to decide whether to close down, the students were there with a paper bag filled with the necessary cash and checks. They informed the board that they wanted to hand it over, but they had a few requests, such as faculty and—heaven forbid—student representation on the Festival board. The board's reaction was typical of educational boards in those days, when college students nationwide were demanding curriculum changes that they thought would better serve them. The EMF board was furious. "We're tired of hearing about student demands." The leader of the students responded, "My friends aren't issuing demands, only suggestions, but if you don't meet them, we'll give the money back to the donors." I watched all this with glee and said not one word, although I was delighted when the board voted to accept their ideas. One longtime member actually voted against accepting this "bribe" and resigned on the spot.

To some extent I suppose most board members and all board presidents want to leave their marks. Some do and in very positive ways. Others simply spin their wheels. And still others actually damage their organization because they decide it needs to be reinvented, which was the case with the EMF board president at the time of my resignation, in 1997, after the Festival had just completed its two most successful seasons in thirty-six years.

Ordinarily, this desire for reinvention is common after a deficit year. Since it is never the board's fault that there is not enough money in the till, there must be something wrong with the program. I've never understood that conclusion, since EMF's formula has remained in essentials the same through good and bad financial times. It's the board that changes.

The 1965 Rockefeller Panel Report, *The Performing Arts: Problems and Prospects*, states:

> Although effective trustees are bound to work continuously with their artistic directors and business managers, they do not meddle in artistic direction and business management. For them there is profound wisdom in the injunction: Do your best to see that the organization is good, that it is well manned, and that it runs smoothly— but do not try to run it.*

---

*Rockefeller Panel, *The Performing Arts: Problems and Prospects* (New York: McGraw-Hill, 1965), 155.

At the end of any year in which EMF faced a deficit the board would look at the largest line item expenditure, which was always the combined musicians' salaries, which is normal with symphony orchestras. And the talk always centered on what we now call downsizing. "We have forty-eight string players in the EPO and sure could save a lot of money by cutting out some of them. Our sixteen first violinists all play the same note. Can't we cut out fifteen of them? And while we're at it, do we really need those three percussionists, since we already have a timpanist? Do we really need the third positions in the flute, oboe, clarinet, bassoon, and trumpet sections, since sometimes they don't even have a part to play?" These are reasonable questions if you don't know much about symphonic repertoire or the makeup of a normal-size orchestra.

In the 1970s the board of a major orchestra, faced with an enormous deficit, engaged an artistic consulting firm, a dangerous way to spend a lot of money. The firm suggested, in total seriousness, that all but one musician in each string section be released and that those who remained be miked so that the electronic sound would make the one player sound like sixteen. What would happen when one of those remaining string players missed a note? Sixteen of the same wrong notes played at the same time would drive the listener, to say nothing of the other musicians, crazy. Fortunately, the board rejected the consultant's recommendation.

There are other problems with reducing an orchestra's size. Historically, there are two types of orchestras: symphony orchestras, with a minimum size of seventy-five musicians, and chamber orchestras, which average between thirty and thirty-five musicians. There is no in-between because composers have rarely written compositions for an orchestra of, say, fifty-five performers. Of course an orchestra can downsize from a symphony orchestra to a chamber orchestra, but the programs will change drastically, and you can bet there will be a tremendous decline in subscription and single-ticket sales. There are very few audiences who will put up with a steady diet of music only by J. S. Bach, Handel, Haydn, and Mozart, with maybe a few minor offerings of Beethoven, Schumann, and Mendelssohn, but almost none of their symphonies or concerti. Any audience will miss the masterpieces, often referred to as warhorses, by such great composers as Brahms, Dvořák, Mahler, Rachmaninoff, Ravel, Richard Strauss, Tchaikovsky, and Wagner, to name but a few.

Those composers and their contemporaries are the ones whose music fills concert halls worldwide. Would an all-Haydn concert attract the same size audience as an all-Beethoven concert? Of course not. Would a concert of offerings by J. S. Bach, Vivaldi, and Mozart attract the same size audience as a concert with works by Ravel, Beethoven, and Tchaikovsky? Never. Since every concertgoer lost represents the loss of a potential contributor, the financial damage to the organization would be devastating.

I am certainly not arguing against chamber orchestras, several of which (the Los Angeles Chamber Orchestra, the McGill Chamber Orchestra in Montreal, the Orchestra of Saint Luke's in New York City, and the Saint Paul Chamber Orchestra, among others) have played an exceedingly important role in North American classical music performance. However, such groups, if they are truly professional, are to be found only in major population centers where there is sufficient interest in my hypothetical J. S. Bach, Vivaldi, and Mozart program and where there is a full-size professional orchestra that can offer the later music.

Actually, I know from the book *The Symphonies of Mozart* (by Georges Poullain, comte de Saint-Foix, 1932) that he was delighted when he had additional string players. Also, I know from research done by Dorothea Baumann, a former president of the International Association of Musicologists, that Handel wrote he was thrilled when he was able to double the size of his string section for the second performance of the *Messiah*. However, tradition has ruled and we seem stuck with the concept of cutting down string sections when a symphony orchestra plays, for example, a Mozart symphony or piano concerto.

The idea of a chamber orchestra trying to play Ravel's *La Valse* or the Brahms Symphony No. 1 is rather like a major league baseball team trying to be competitive while playing with no outfielders. By the time that team is 0–15 at the end of the first inning of the season's first game, there won't be any fans willing to stay or buy tickets to any other games.

NINE

What a Conductor Does

THE WIFE OF A GOOD FRIEND AND AN EMF BOARD MEMBER kids me about the uselessness of conductors. Says Debby, "When you're conducting I look at the orchestra members and they aren't paying the slightest attention to you. They're looking only at the music." Actually, I prefer to tell people that all you have to do in this business is strut out to the podium, face the audience, bow, turn around, give a down beat, continue waving the baton until the musicians stop playing, turn around, face the audience, bow, and then exit.

I find it interesting but not surprising that the French word for baton is baguette, the same as for the bread. For the French, great food is revered at least as much as great technique with the baton. Oops. Baguette.

Banking on the assumption that there's a wannabe conductor lurking behind just about every music lover, in 1990 I borrowed a brilliant idea from a few other orchestras and introduced an amateur conducting competition at EMF. Anyone who wanted could conduct the orchestra for seven minutes. The only requirement was payment of a fee of one thousand dollars. The orchestra agreed to donate its services for one night, and I selected the music, which consisted of works the orchestra could play in its sleep. Some of the conductors hammed it up and spoofed the event, others took it more seriously. They waved their arms and at the end of the program the winner was determined by applause meter. It turned out to be a relatively painless way to raise money, and everyone seemed to have fun.

Dr. Sam LeBauer, when he was board president, entered the competition, to the delight of the orchestra members. After he finished trying to conduct Mozart's *Marriage of Figaro* he said to me, "That was harder than any medical exam I ever had to take."

I have always told my students never to confuse the podium with a trampoline, sometimes to no avail. I always get a kick out of hearing the New York Philharmonic old-timers talk about how subdued Leonard Bernstein's conducting motions were before television began broadcasting his concerts. A few years ago I engaged for EMF a European conductor whose English was as slight as his gestures were large. He was rehearsing a composition that included a saxophone in the instrumentation. At one point during the rehearsal he turned to the sax player and said, "I need more sex." The quip—he clearly knew what he was saying—really cracked up the musicians, although they soon tired of dealing with yet another dancing conductor.

All an orchestral musician really wants and needs is to see the tip of the baton (to know exactly what the beat is, the phrasing desired, and the dynamic level), the eyes of the person on the podium (to be certain of entrances and intensity), and in rehearsal to hear as few nonmusical words as possible. At the performance the last thing the orchestra member wants is to have to guess what part of the anatomy of the conductor to look at for a cue or phrase.

There is an interesting paragraph along these lines in the autobiography of Walter Damrosch, the esteemed music director of what was then called the New York Symphony Orchestra. In describing the 1877 debut performance of Richard Wagner's *Parsifal*, Damrosch writes:

> I was naturally much interested in the invisible, subterranean orchestra of the Bayreuth auditorium, and as the first noble theme of the prelude literally floated into the darkened hall, the great advan-

tage of an invisible conductor was manifest . . . and I still wish it were possible to educate the public to listen to music with their ears only and not with their eyes. But this theory of mine would find violent opposition from the company of "prima donna conductors" who, at that parting of the ways which comes to every conductor, whether he shall make himself an interpreter of the composer's works or a perverter in order to demonstrate his own "tricks of the trade," have chosen the primrose path because a large part of the public are easily gulled and more easily moved if the conductor "dramatizes" the music through his gestures. By the skillful manipulation of his arms and hands, his hips and his hair, he gives the impression that when the 'cellos play a soulful melody, it really drips from his wrists. . . .

There are many people, especially among the gentle sex, to whom admiration for one conductor entails a deep hatred of all others. It would be interesting to note how many of them could pick out their favorite if half a dozen of the prima donnas of the baton were to perform invisibly with an invisible orchestra in quick succession to each other.*

It is interesting to watch television documentaries about famous conductors of the past. Most of them (Szell, Reiner, Bernstein, and Toscanini, to name but a few) were slight in physical stature, many being under five and a half feet tall. A tall conductor is at a disadvantage because he must bend down to maintain eye contact with the musicians and to keep the baton at a level where the players can have the best possible view of its tip.

I have told all my students not to play to the audience, but to work *with* the orchestra. I also pass on Gunther Schuller's advice that when something goes wrong in rehearsal think first of what you might have done that caused the problem before correcting a section or individual player. It is highly likely that the cause of the problem was on the podium. And always remember that the baton doesn't make any sound. Some stu-

*Walter Damrosch, *My Musical Life* (New York: Scribner's, 1940), 45–46.

dents listened, some didn't. As for dancing conductors, from the point of view of most musicians, they are almost worse than no conductor at all.

Most musicians will agree that rehearsals are much more enjoyable than concerts. The concert, the production, is simply a result of what went on in the rehearsals. I've never bought the idea that a bad dress rehearsal means a good concert. Everyone is either prepared or not—and that includes the conductor. I am a fiend for detail and am of the opinion that the conductor is no more important to the end result than the back-row second violinist. We're all in this together.

Great coaches understand the value of preparation. In the fall of 1981 I wrote a letter to someone I had come to admire, Dean E. Smith, then head basketball coach at the University of North Carolina. I said that it seemed to me that what we did was not very different. What he called practices in preparation for games I called rehearsals in preparation for concerts. Although I knew that his practices were private, I asked if it might be possible for me to attend them for one week prior to his opening game of the 1981–82 season and speak to him about similarities of our jobs after each one. Dean wrote that he found the idea intriguing and that there would be a pass for me at the basketball office that week.

Dean Smith is the finest teacher I ever encountered in any discipline. His organizational skills, his eagerness to teach, his ability to be as quick with praise as with positive constructive criticism, and his willingness to let several things go wrong before stopping to make corrections were all utterly fascinating. He spent as much time working with those who would have little opportunity to play as he did with Michael Jordan—a freshman that year. I made copious notes during the practices and when we spoke, Dean seemed surprised that I felt I was learning so much from him. The fact that he won more "concerts" than any coach in college basketball history before his retirement should not have been a surprise to anyone who knew him. Each year after 1982 I invited him to give a master class at EMF on motivation and preparation, an invitation he always declined. He is not a public man and detests giving speeches even more than I. However, he always asked for my conducting schedule, and he gave me tickets to some of UNC's games. Whoever first coined the phrase "a gentleman and a scholar" had to have known there would eventually be someone like Dean Smith. I am a much better conductor for having watched him teach.

(As an aside, a game of hoops means more to me with each passing year, since all you have to do is shoot, without moving around a lot and getting too much exercise. The primary problem, at least at my current age, is that from year to year the rim seems to get a few inches higher. Not long ago I spent one summer evening losing one game of H-O-R-S-E after another to Wynton Marsalis and James Jenkins, a great friend and tuba player. I wondered then how Wynton had found time to perfect his shot. On second thought, perhaps I needed to spend more time shooting hoops and less time studying scores.)

◆ DURING MY LAST SEVERAL SUMMERS AT EMF THE TWO student orchestra conductors, my assistant conductor, and I had a two-hour session with all the instrumental students the night before their first rehearsal. One of the numerous items we discussed was that conductors spend about three-fourths of orchestral rehearsal time, regardless of performing level, concentrating on the string players, since they literally have hundreds more notes to play than do the woodwinds, percussion, harp, or brass. Our instructions were that during rehearsals the non-string players should continue to focus their attention on what the conductor was saying because they could learn a lot from listening to the entire picture. Of course, if you go to a professional rehearsal you will probably see (especially from trombone, tuba, and percussion sections) players reading everything from the daily newspaper to a mystery novel. The result is that when the conductor is finished with the strings and wants to rehearse the brass or percussions, precious moments are lost as the section re-acclimates itself to the music. The students natually saw this when they had occasion to witness the EPO in rehearsal. How to stop it? You can't.

During rehearsals, the EPO is far better behaved than most groups. The New York Philharmonic and the Philadelphia Orchestra have the worst reputations for behaving childishly, especially with guest conductors. At his request, I once went to two weeks of rehearsals led by the distinguished German conductor Eugen Jochum when he was giving some concerts with the New York Philharmonic. The "children" went to work almost immediately at the first rehearsal, passing notes, shooting paper clips, and—worse—mimicking Jochum's left-hand motions when he was looking in another direction. I felt as though I were watching a kindergarten class. What I didn't realize was that Jochum knew all the time exactly what was happening and decided that only through his superior music-making could he put a stop to it. He reached a place in the score of Brahms's Symphony No. 4 where there is a famous solo passage for the principal flute, a passage the flutist Julius Baker had performed perhaps a thousand times. Jochum singled him out and rehearsed him alone for at least five minutes. The Philharmonic members were indignant—how dare anyone presume to rehearse one of their most famous and best players? But they couldn't argue it on musical grounds: Jochum was absolutely correct in his reteaching. Baker had probably taken this solo for granted for several decades and he was doing it wrong.

◙ IF YOU LOOK AT THE SO-CALLED BIG FIVE ORCHESTRAS IN the United States, which have a combined history of about six hundred years, only one of them has ever had a music director who was born *and* trained in the States. That was Leonard Bernstein and his tenure with the New York Philharmonic was eleven years.

Why is this the case? Because we don't have nearly as many professional orchestras and, especially, opera houses for apprenticeships, and our training is theoretical and usually anything but hands-on. To make matters worse, most of our conservatories and schools of music seem determined to equate conducting ability with a doctorate of musical arts (DMA).

Most of my colleagues are outraged when I tell them they're not getting the best jobs because they have not been as well prepared as the Europeans. But the young European conductor has probably already given several public performances of the Beethoven Symphony No. 3 before his or her North American counterpart even begins studying this work. I liken it to playing the violin—holding the violin between your left arm and neck is awkward and uncomfortable, but much more so for a fifteen-year-old than six-year-old beginner. For the latter it soon becomes second nature.

Every five years at EMF we asked the orchestra members to rate by secret ballot all our guest conductors. The last time we did this, the top four were all Europeans, with the next eleven (Americans and Canadians) lagging far behind.

◙ THE GREATEST NATIVE NORTH AMERICAN PIANIST WE have known, the Canadian Glenn Gould, wrote an interesting article in 1962, which was reprinted in the publication *Musical America*.* The title was "Let's Ban Applause!" and shortly after it appeared he retired entirely from public performance. Gould argues that performers shouldn't need applause, which he calls "demonstrations," at the conclusion of a performance in order to derive satisfaction from their work. Anyone who has conducted or played in a radio broadcast, where there is no applause, understands that the satisfaction of a good performance comes from within. In addition, too much applause can lead to something I detest almost as much as playing national anthems—encores.

But anthems are the worst. I recall a moment just before a concert I was conducting in Hamilton, Ontario. The manager said, "And don't forget that we always start with *O Canada*." I said, "What? I've never even heard it before. Get me a score, fast." Of course, they didn't have one, but the librarian rushed back to his office, got me a first violin part, and prevented what would have been an embarrassing situation. The fact is I've never understood what anthems have to do with Beethoven, Brahms, or Bartók.

A very disagreeable situation arose with the Harrisburg Symphony Orchestra in 1991. About five minutes before the concert was to begin the manager knocked on my dressing room door and said, "Thank God! The war has started, and the board president and I want you to open with the national anthem." When I declined she told me that she had anticipated my response and that if I didn't conduct it the assistant con-

---

*Glenn Gould, "Let's Ban Applause!" *Musical America* (February 1962), 245–47.

ductor would. The music director was not in town, and there was no telephone in the dressing room to call him to discuss the situation. I did conduct it. I thought about telling the audience that I was doing so under protest but decided that would just make matters worse. Had this happened with my own orchestra, I would have absolutely refused. However, in this situation I was the guest. Some of the musicians refused to play, holding their instruments on their laps, and others purposely played incorrect notes. What I didn't know was that two of the musicians had brothers already stationed in the Persian Gulf. Conducting the anthem that night is not something I'm proud of.

◘ I WAS IN TORONTO ONCE FOR A SERIES OF CONCERTS, AND the soloist for one concert was a soprano faculty member at the Toronto Conservatory. After rehearsal one day I took her to lunch and for some reason the conversation turned to Glenn Gould. She had gone to school with him and said that all the stories of his idiosyncracies were true, that indeed his parents had sent him to school in a heavy coat that he wore all day in temperatures of seventy to eighty degrees, and that even back then he never ate at the cafeteria lest he somehow be contaminated by food or water that was not fresh. At that time, even though I was well aware that Gould had stopped performing in public, I dreamed of having him come to EMF under whatever conditions he would accept, and my soloist friend was kind enough to give me his unlisted phone number and address. I wrote him a letter, sent him some Festival materials, and for the next six months or so I'd dial his number whenever I had an idle moment.

One day he actually answered the phone, and I was so shocked that I didn't know what to say. It didn't matter, because the one thing that Gould could do faster than play the piano was talk. He quickly told me he had my letter and the materials in his study, apologized for not having answered, and launched into an hour-long explication of the entire history of the Viennese school of composition. I just listened, marveling at his intellect. Of course the only other option was to hang up. Peter Ostwald, a psychiatrist and a musician, wrote a fascinating biography of Gould and in one passage stated: "His vocal exuberance seemed like some kind of primal experience, a joyous discharge of emotion and intellect, mockery and fantasy, all designed to fascinate if not dominate the listener."* Ostwald must have known him well. In our conversation, after Gould finally came up for air, I asked whether he would be willing to appear at EMF and under what conditions. He said, "No problem. I've been thinking about it and I'd like to perform the Schoenberg Piano Concerto. Also, I've carefully calculated that it will take exactly thirteen full rehearsals before the performance, at which, of course, there can't be an audience." I told him I'd be back in touch. Somehow I knew the board wouldn't accept those conditions, nor would the musicians. As for me, I think it would have been great fun. Except I don't like that particular concerto.

◙ APPROACHING A SCORE FOR THE FIRST OR ONE HUNDRED and first time is an awesome experience. I get very nervous because of my responsibility to the composer. It's as if he or she is looking over my shoulder demanding that I convey the essence of the piece. I had a lengthy conversation about this with Joe Gingold, who followed up with a letter in which he wrote, "Conductors must always adhere to the written text but never feel chained by it." Shortly afterward, in September 1991, I relayed this quote to Gunther Schuller, who responded with the following:

> I had already suggested in my earlier letter that there may be little difference between what Gingold says and means, and what I mean. It is perhaps a question of semantics, or rather what exactly he intends his words to convey. For me they were too general to be specific and clear, and therefore allowed for a range of interpretations.
>
> Take your sentence: ". . . adhering strictly to the text would obviously make of us automatons." That is not necessarily true; it is, in my view, an untenable assumption, the accuracy of which will depend on: 1) the quality of the "adhering to the text" that is being

---

*Peter Ostwald, *Glenn Gould: The Ecstasy and Tragedy of Genius* (New York: W. W. Norton, 1997), 27–28.

done, and 2) what precisely is meant by the words "adhering strictly." If by "adhering strictly" is meant some accurate but dull, mechanical, unimaginative, uninspired rendering of the text, then it will be the work of an automaton. If, on the other hand, someone follows, say, Brahms' meticulous, explicit, precise notations and with those, i.e. *from* those, derives, without abandoning those notational instructions, an expressive, spontaneous sounding, imaginative, inspired performance, then it will *not* be the work of an automaton. It is not *what* we do as conductors but *how*: how we interpret or realize the information in the score. And for me the whole range from ignoring to misinterpreting that information is simply not acceptable nor desirable.

The little "cosmetic" interpretations you mention in your letter are, *of course*, allowable and appropriate. Not only that, they are probably *unavoidable* by living, breathing human beings. It is therefore a matter of degree, a matter of taste, a matter of balance, and a matter of respect for the score and the information in it.

I put that letter in my briefcase and reread it at least once a month. In my opinion it is an extraordinary document. Nobody has ever said it as well.

T E N

The Real Job: Music Director

IN A RECENT *NEW YORK TIMES* ARTICLE BERNARD HOLLAND
wrote:

> Another breed of conductor is the music director, the one with the
> permanent job. Making music, especially in this country, is only
> part of it. American music directors are administrators, hirers, firers
> (though these days with difficulty), planners, glad-handers, money-
> raisers, politicians and donor strokers. Good teeth and a mellow
> voice are assets. What a vast occupation it is: the conductor as C.E.O.,
> professor, psychiatrist, public-relations officer, and a ballet dancer.*

I think there is more room for fraud in choosing a music director than
in any other post in the performing arts because selection committees
are looking for and attracted more to nonmusical qualifications than

---

*Bernard Holland, "Making Music by Sleight of Hand and Eye," *New York Times*,
August 13, 1995, Arts and Leisure sect., 23.

musical ones. In the past year I have had inside knowledge of two criteria lists for music director posts in North America. Each list had ten items, one finally included the word "music" on item six, the other on item seven. Dancing and wildly waving one's arms while conducting did not appear on either list but it can be *the* make or break if, in fact, there are auditions for a position. The only thing that can equal such an "attribute" is to have, or at least try to fake, a foreign accent during the interview process.

As the story was later told to me, a graduate school student I had known at Florida State obtained the music directorship of the Jacksonville Symphony Orchestra through clever but devious means. As soon as the opening was announced he phoned a friend in London and another in Paris to assist in his plan. Then he set up a luncheon with the Jacksonville search committee. He made certain that the restaurant had a moveable telephone (cordless ones were not yet on the scene). While the salad was being served their waiter appeared with the telephone and announced that the Maestro had an urgent call from his "agent" in Paris. During dessert the waiter returned with yet another call, this time from his "agent" in London. The search committee was sufficiently impressed and offered him the position without ever having seen him conduct. He was fired after two seasons.

In 1984 I conducted a concert with the Mississippi State Symphony. They fired their music director at the end of that season and offered me the position. I told them I wasn't interested, although I did agree to act as interim music director for one year while they had a search. Part of the agreement was that I would conduct the first and last concerts of their 1985–86 season and would act as an ex-officio member of the search committee. This entailed narrowing down to ten the list of candidates I thought suitable. More than two hundred people applied. Remember, *everybody* is a conductor.

I agreed not only to travel to Jackson for the dress rehearsal and concert of each person they chose to guest conduct, but also to have a one-on-one interview with each candidate. I arrived two days before the first rehearsal for the opening concert and had a productive session with the search committee. The only difficulty was getting them to agree to have the orchestra represented on the committee, but finally they assented.

The next day I spent a few hours with the executive director, who tried to get me to side with him against the union requests for higher pay. He was wasting his time: I've spent a good deal of my life fighting for better pay and working conditions for symphony orchestra musicians. The morning of the first rehearsal the executive director telephoned me at my hotel to tell me his good news: "The orchestra has threatened to strike, but the board has backed me and we're locking them out." This man and most of the board were actually pleased that no music would be played, at least for a while. Because of the three-month lockout I had to reschedule all the concerts for the candidates and rearrange my EMF off-season work.

But the search continued. After the last candidate had performed I had the orchestra members vote by secret ballot for their favorite conductor. It turned out that their overwhelming favorite was the same as the search committee's, and the Irishman Colman Pearce was named to the position. Two weeks after the announcement was made in the newspaper, I had a call from one of the other candidates wondering about the status of the search. The committee had not had the common decency to notify those who had not been selected.

◙ THE MOST DIFFICULT PART OF THE JOB FOR THE CONSCIentious, hands-on music director is programming. At EMF I had one self-imposed rule: no repetitions of any piece performed in public concerts within a three-year period. This included solo, chamber music, and orchestral works. My rationale was that some students would attend the festival for three consecutive seasons, and I wanted each "listening" experience to be something new. Trying to plan the EPO and the two student orchestras was difficult primarily because of the third woodwinds, tuba, percussion, and harp. I had to be certain there was at least one major composition for the students of those instruments to play each week. I also considered the duration of every concert, setting (with rare exceptions) a seventy-five-minute maximum of actual music for a ninety-minute performance. This takes into account the number of minutes involved in moving a piano onstage, the anticipated duration of applause, as well as tuning and hesitations between movements of a multimovement composition, all of which can easily add ten or more minutes of nonperformance time to a concert.

In 1980 David Daniels did a great favor for all music directors when he published his *Orchestral Music*, a book with average timings, instrumentation, nationalities of composers, and publishers of all major compositions. In 1996 he recompiled the information for a third edition. If you need to find a seventeen-minute composition for strings, triple winds except English horn, four trumpets, no trombones or tuba, timpani, and harp by a nineteenth-century Russian composer, the Daniels book can do it for you in minutes. It is that well organized and cross-referenced.

Programming for the professional chamber music series was always a nightmare for me. I asked for input from all orchestra members, soliciting suggestions that included instrumentation and timings. Likewise, I wrote to each guest artist and asked that he or she send me a list of five possibilities, all of which had to be checked against what had been performed the previous three seasons. Confirming the final selections (which may not have been on the lists submitted) with the guest artists was always difficult, since the artists were so often on tour and, as always seemed to be the case, would not be returning until such time as I myself would be on tour! To further complicate matters, I needed to put into the mix those members of our faculty whose sound I thought would best balance that of the artist. It was also important that as many of our faculty as possible perform *something* on this six-concert series.

Another wrinkle resulted when, from time to time, a faculty member would suggest a chamber work that I would then program—but I did not assign that person to perform the piece because I didn't feel that he or she was right for it. I certainly didn't please all the people all the time. I probably didn't even please 60 percent of the people 60 percent of the time.

Being a North American music director today requires going to board, staff, and committee meetings, making fund-raising calls, giving interviews, making television and radio appearances, and attending to the numerous other details of artistic administration. In most orchestras today the back-row second violinist has more time to practice than the music director has to study. If he or she had as much time to study as the violinist has to practice, many orchestras would be substantially better.

ELEVEN

The Pressure Cooker

Auditioning is nerve-wracking and one of the toughest experiences a musician faces. Each year at EMF I gave a master class titled "On Audition Procedures," which was basically a grocery list of "do's" and "don'ts." Among the suggestions was one that may seem obvious—be sure of your references. I included that one because I knew a very talented violinist who kept getting denied even the chance to audition. It turned out that one of her references was critical (wrongly) of her playing and attitude, squelching any chance she might have had of winning a position. An additional precaution: do some research. In another case a fine cellist kept getting the positions he wanted, but the orchestras he worked for continued to go bankrupt. If he had checked the financial status of those ensembles he wouldn't have considered taking a position with them. Other suggestions: don't use the warm-up room to try to impress the other applicants; know exactly how each orchestral excerpt fits into everything else that is going on in the score; play exactly what is asked and not one note more; never request a tempo, because doing so can give the impression of your not being prepared; and try in the solo selection to find some way to "stand out" from the crowd because the jury will be listening to maybe fifty people that day.

Taking auditions is not only terrifying, it is also very expensive, and most organizations do little to lessen the cost for the participants. At Eastern Music Festival we, like many other orchestras, invited a limited number of people to audition after we received and reviewed their résumés. For example, for a principal wind opening we would receive perhaps 150 applications, from which a maximum of twenty would be asked to audition. Over the years I became astute at reading applications and it became easier to identify those who were not qualified. The most obvious red flags were too little experience with a professional orchestra and no teaching affiliation with a major school. If the applicant seemed marginal and had to travel a long distance, we did not invite him or her. Why have someone spend hundreds of dollars for an airplane trip, hotel room, taxis, and meals when I knew from the bio that he or she really had little chance of winning? It's even worse for cellists and double bassists who have to pay for an extra airplane ticket for their instruments.

I'll never forget a discussion a few faculty members and I had in 1983 with our artist-in-residence Gunther Schuller when he was still music director at the Tanglewood Festival. It was well past midnight, and as Gunther was downing yet another Big Mac, he declared that I was easily the second best in the business at reading between the lines on résumés— the clear implication being that he was the best. When we laughed he didn't. I don't think he understood the inference.

A pet peeve I have with most orchestras is that they have auditions on weekdays, making it impossible for the musicians to take advantage of the airlines' Saturday overnight discounts. Weekday tickets cost up to four times more. This scheduling is usually done because it is more convenient for the judges. At the Festival we tried to have the bulk of our auditions on Saturdays and Sundays.

Of course, the major expense musicians face, besides their years of training, are their instruments. Conductors get off easy. A good baton costs about twenty dollars today. A decent violin can easily run to ten thousand times that.

◙ DO SEXISM AND RACISM PLAY ROLES IN SELECTING MEM-
bers for North American orchestras? Absolutely. Many years ago music
directors refused to engage females because "what happens to them each
month might affect their performing." As for African Americans or
American Indians, until fairly recently they (with the exception of some
fabulous vocalists) were simply not considered as participants in mainstream classical music. In the 1960s, when government guidelines were
being issued against discriminatory employment, most orchestras began
to audition applicants behind a screen. Each musician was given a number for his or her order in the auditions, and the judges couldn't see who
was female or African American. My opinion is that this worked until
judges figured out ways to beat the system. For example, a judge will immediately recognize an auditioning musician if it is one of his or her students because of the style of phrasing and the sound. When one hundred
applicants are narrowed down to four semifinalists everybody involved
knows who those people are, and if one or more of them happen to be
black or female they face the same obstacles they do in many professions—all other things being equal, the white male gets the job almost
every time.

In recent years I have had numerous musicians tell me that they would
prefer, on musical grounds, not to have to play behind a screen because
being able to see your "audience" encourages you to perform better simply because of the visual contact with human beings. Besides, who wants
to be a number?

◙ I AM OFTEN ASKED WHETHER, TO THE BEST OF MY KNOWL-
edge, artists are more involved in sex and drugs than people who work
in other arenas. Yes. Except for, I suspect, professional athletes. When
pitcher Jim Bouton wrote his "tell-all" book *Ball Four* about the lives
of professional baseball players, the baseball establishment went bon-
kers. But Bouton was right on the mark, especially when he wrote about
performance-enhancing drugs that only made the player *think* he was
doing great.

In 1979 I agreed to participate in a series of stress tests on performing
artists. The organization, MedMedia, sent down their crew from New

York City—two video cameramen, a producer, and a director—who followed me around for four days. They monitored me in rehearsal, out of rehearsal, teaching classes, eating meals with the students—everything up to, and including, sitting at my desk studying scores. About every hour or so the producer would take my pulse and blood pressure.

During a discussion with the whole crew at breakfast one morning I learned the name of the person who had scored highest in their tests, the person who was most stressed out before going on stage: Johnny Carson. A few years later, on Carson's next-to-last show, the cameras panned the backstage area for about five minutes. There was Carson pacing frantically back and forth before he made his entrance for one of his wonderfully entertaining monologues, during which he always seemed so utterly relaxed.

All professional performing musicians experience some degree of stage fright. For most of us it disappears within seconds of the start of the concert or audition. However, it is now possible for anyone to play without a shaky bow or mouthpiece or baton.

The drugs of the day for orchestral performers are beta blockers, and their use is rampant, at least in North America. I have been told by a member of the Chicago Symphony Orchestra that more than 75 percent of their players take them, and that even though they are prescription drugs, they are easier to obtain than a Cuban cigar. Beta blockers apparently lower the blood pressure without affecting muscle coordination. But the reported side effects of impotency and fatigue would stop me from taking them. More important, this medication tends to remove the spontaneity required for beautiful music-making. My guess is that the use of beta blockers began, in part, in reaction to pressure for perfect (in terms of notes) performances and recordings. Because of perfection in CD recordings, our classical music public has come to expect the same in the concert hall.

I still enjoy the great 1950s LP recording of the Brahms Symphony No. 2 by the Royal Concertgebouw Orchestra of Amsterdam, in which the tuba player misses an important note. At that time there was more concern for the overall performance, since it would have been easy enough to re-record that section, which was near the end of the piece. And what was so terrible about the "splat" on the high C made by the great Phil Farkas, who told me that if he ever got to the point where he felt he had to take any drug before a performance, he would get out of the business.

The Rubinsteins of old were concerned mainly with musical integrity and the beauty demanded by the composer. There is a story about an interview with Arthur Rubinstein after a concert. The fabled pianist said that a good composer could have written a sonata made up of all the wrong notes he had just played. Rubinstein wasn't advocating mediocrity, nor am I. It just seems to me that conveying the artistic message to the audience should always come first. Nobody knocks in the three-pointer every time. Not even Michael Jordan—except when the whole shebang is on the line, and I'd be willing to bet the farm that he never took any kind of drug.

As for sexual harassment, I know of several conductors who have taken advantage of their musicians. The most outrageous example is of a gifted and rising young conductor who often threatened female musicians with dismissal unless they would sleep with him. He eventually lost his position, but not for sexual harassment! Rather, his bar, restaurant, and clothing store debts became such an embarrassment to the board that it voted to release him. Another was a mediocre conductor who took advantage of females in his orchestra. That man also lost his job, again not for harassment, but because of his lack of musicianship.

Conductors often attain a kind of power much like that of the super-star athlete or the charismatic politician (though usually not so considerable!). Those who take advantage of that power should receive a punishment far more serious than simply being fired.

◙ I ALWAYS FOUND FIRING PEOPLE ONE OF THE MOST STRESS-ful things I had to do. Through confidential student and faculty questionnaires I was often able to identify changes that needed to be made in our faculty. On one occasion I learned that a harp teacher was being verbally abusive. I immediately had the personnel manager step in and was ready to follow up quickly if it was necessary. It was. I fired her.

What was far more difficult was to see some member of the faculty falter after a number of years. The procedure we developed for dealing with the situation was, I think, as fair and just as could be. When I felt that the teaching or performing of any faculty member was sliding downhill I usually had the personnel manager meet with that person and then, if there didn't seem to be improvement, I would meet with the two of them. For example, EMF once had a tuba player who fell into this category. When we met to discuss his performance he said that he frankly was no longer interested in the position, that he was continuing only because of the prestige and performing opportunities. That was easy to deal with. Adios.

The two toughest decisions I ever had to make regarding faculty dealt with student orchestra conductors. One of these had been a friend at Brevard, and he had played a large role in the founding of the Festival. The agreement he and I reached after about ten years was that he wasn't doing his best work, and so he should take a year's leave of absence. But when he returned nothing had really changed, and I was frankly outraged when I went to one of his concerts that included the *Adagietto* from the Mahler Symphony No. 5. Because he was having so many problems in rehearsals, he made a cut in the most difficult passage, thus eliminating almost a third of the movement. That was it for me. He had insulted the intelligence and abilities of our students, and I released him after that season. The student orchestras over the years have played beautifully such difficult works as the Mahler Symphonies No. 3 and No. 6, *Petruchka*, the Beethoven Symphony No. 9, Bartók's Concerto for Orchestra, and Debussy's *La Mer*, just to give a few examples. I was not willing to be a party to playing down to them by insinuating that they were not capable of playing the entire *Adagietto*. The interesting thing is that not only did he understand my decision but also we remained friends for years. When I resigned from EMF he sent me an e-mail that said in part, "You have made an enormous impact on the lives of many, many young musicians and I am pleased that I was able to have been a part of the enterprise in the early years." It takes a person with a generous heart to have written that.

The other student conductor I released was a superior educator at the time I hired him, but he became generally more and more bitter about life and simply was not able to grow with changing times, musically and otherwise. He began to bring his anger into the rehearsal hall. Although some faculty had complained to me and students had written about it in their questionnaires for some years, I protected him—because he was such a close personal friend. I should have talked to him at least five years before I released him. That I didn't do so was foolish, cowardly, and detrimental to many students.

TWELVE

All Aboard!

Oটher than my work with emf, i have conducted much more often in Europe, Canada, and South America than in the United States. It all began in 1967, when my manager called to inform me of a guest-conducting tour in Europe. "You wouldn't believe how difficult it was to arrange this but, with my connections, this is only the beginning of a great European career for you." In fact, he was mostly correct, except for the bit about "his connections."

There were three engagements on the initial trip, one with the Bucharest State Philharmonic, preceded by a concert in the smallish Romanian city of Tîrgu-Mureş (the Romanian government wanted to get the most out of me—there was no additional pay for Tîrgu-Mureş, but that was a condition of the invitation for the State Philharmonic), and a recording in London of an all-Mozart program.

My friend John Semivan from my NEC days was then writing for the *Detroit Free Press*, and when I told him about the tour he got the paper to assign him to do a story about the arts in eastern Europe. We took the same transatlantic flight, and as we arrived at Charles de Gaulle Airport

John looked out the window and said, "Look at those airport workers, they're all communists working for a better France." But the real kicker was when we landed in Bucharest. In those days international passengers had to walk about two hundred yards into the airport customs area. As we started the trek I saw a gaggle of television cameras. It was clear to me that I had arrived, that the great art-loving public in Bucharest had to find out everything they could about the young American maestro. I gave my best pose and prepared for a general press conference, until all the media folk marched right past me to get what they could from another passenger on the plane, Arthur Ashe.

But the Hotel Transylvania, which still exists, awaited me in Tîrgu-Mureş (now for some reason spelled Târgu-Mureş). My translator was Harold Oyntzen, a flute player whose Boris Karloff accent was right out of central casting. After a few days I asked Harold if he knew of any of the Hollywood films about Count Dracula, and was there really any truth to the story. He said, "Oh, zumtimes peasants talk but iz really nahthing."

In Tîrgu-Mureş, John and I were flabbergasted to see a fully professional orchestra, opera, and theater, all subsidized by what was even then quite a poor country. The director of the entire operation was a composer named Csiky Boldizsár. I became friends with Csiky and the orchestra and returned five times. Sadly, I had to postpone a May 1999 appearance at a Beethoven festival there because of the war in Kosovo. What this orchestra lacked in the quality of their instruments was more than made up for by their wonderful string players, their pride, and their musicianship.

I met Csiky the day of my first rehearsal. He had told Harold to bring me to his office when we were finished, and once there, Csiky motioned for me to take a seat. Within a few moments there was a knock on the door. A soprano and the conductor of the opera entered, took their seats at opposite ends of a large table, and started screaming at each other just as Csiky joined them. He let the yelling continue for about five minutes, at which point he slammed his fist on the table, which certainly got everyone's attention, and said a few words in a soft voice. The soprano and conductor quietly exited. Csiky then went to his desk, drew a picture of a boat, fishing rods, and beer bottles, handed them to me, and said, "Okay?" We didn't catch many fish that afternoon but the beer was terrific—and so is Csiky.

With the Bucharest Philharmonic I knew that I would face a hostile group of seasoned and excellent musicians just waiting to pounce on a young upstart conductor. This is always the case with the number-one group in every major city, as I later discovered in Dublin, Budapest, and Toronto. But I did have an advantage in this instance, because the program was a Haydn cello concerto and the Mahler Symphony No. 5, which the orchestra had never before played. Taking a page out of Fred Prausnitz's book, I began the first rehearsal in the middle of a fiendishly difficult passage in the *Scherzo* movement of the Mahler, not giving any of the orchestra members the slightest opportunity to challenge me, because they had to scramble just to try to play the notes.

In Bucharest a youngish cellist invited John and me to his home for dinner the next evening for a traditional Romanian dish. Just before rehearsal the following day he told me that the powers-that-be had learned of the invitation, and he was told to rescind it. It was one thing to invite a Jew to conduct an orchestra but quite another to have one over for a meal.

As John and I flew from the Bucharest airport for the London recording he turned to me and said, "Workers of the world should take a bath at least once in a while." We both had a good laugh, but it took fourteen more years before an electrician at the Gdańsk Ship Yard in Poland would jump over a fence out of pure frustration and begin a great social upheaval that, among other things, improved personal hygiene.

Observing other cultures and meeting people who are interested in matters other than music make guest conducting in non–North American cities especially stimulating. In October 1990 I was rehearsing in the East German city of Rostock when it was announced that the divided Germany would be reunited. The announcement was made during a break, and according to the manager, most of the musicians were too stunned to believe it.

In 1991 I received an invitation to conduct the Czech National Radio Orchestra, quite an honor—though short-lived. About three weeks before I was to leave for Prague I received a phone call from the manager of the station's music division. He told me that the orchestra had just been invited to substitute for another orchestra's tour, that I would still be conducting the same program in Prague at the same fee, but with the orchestra from Pardubice. So I flew to Prague, was driven to Pardubice, and spent several days in that lovely city while I rehearsed a quite good ensemble.

The morning of the concert I took a very early train to Prague and checked into an enormous, monolithic hotel that the communists had no doubt considered sumptuous. Some friends (including a former student of mine from EMF) came to talk and have coffee in the morning. Afterward I went up to my room, which was *really* cold. I telephoned the receptionist, who said, "There's nothing to worry about; wait until the afternoon when the sun is shining in the direction of your room and things will warm up quickly." I spent that day under the covers. Despite what most people say, Smetana Hall is not that great acoustically. But it is heated.

From 1980 to 1984 I was principal guest conductor in Seville. I had previously conducted a concert there, my first of many in Spain, and the contract said that the morning rehearsals would begin between 11:00 and 11:30, which I quickly learned meant that we would start only after all the musicians had arrived. During the break in that first rehearsal some of the players asked if I wanted to join them at the bar. As I enjoyed my coffee they threw back several glasses of wine or cognac, which is why the second part of rehearsals in Spain are especially challenging for the conductor.

Largely because of a wise colleague, Edmon Colomer, Spanish orchestras have greatly improved since the beginning of the 1990s. Edmon, a native of Barcelona and an immensely gifted musician, was tired of seeing so many non-Spaniards in the orchestras there. In an attempt to solve the problem, Edmon established the National Youth Orchestra of Spain (JONDE) to give young people the orchestral training that was not then offered at the conservatories in Spain. Because of his efforts, many of the graduates of his program now hold important positions in Spanish orchestras. I conducted the JONDE for two concerts in 1991 and witnessed firsthand that Edmon was just as concerned about musical education as he was about having a great professional career.

Rehearsals and concerts in France are not much different from those in Spain except that having a large number of foreigners in a French orchestra would create a scandal of sizeable proportions. The French are absolutely convinced that their musicians, especially those trained in Paris, are the world's greatest. However, the work ethic in Spain and France is much the same.

The best orchestras I have ever conducted are eastern European, where the string playing is certainly on a level with the best orchestras in western Europe and North America. My times with the Budapest Opera Orchestra remain memorable experiences for me, although after the fall of communism all my contacts there were released from their positions, and I have not been re-engaged. I remember a performance of the Bruckner Symphony No. 5 with them that was so astonishing that I almost wished someone else had been conducting so I could relax and listen. I also recall that after that concert there was the usual stream of youngsters waiting backstage for my autograph, a common practice in Europe. As I was busy signing, I looked up and saw a large woman in a heavy fur coat bearing down on me. I wasn't embarrassed until she opened her mouth and loudly announced, "I'm from Dayton and I think your concert was just wonderful."

The finest ensemble I've ever worked with is the Sinfonia Varsovia. That group includes most of the best players in Poland, but they are constantly on tour and seldom perform in their own country. Even the Paris critics love them. The last time I worked with them was in Germany, and the program was the Stravinsky *Pulcinella Suite*, Spohr's Violin Concerto No. 8, and the Beethoven Symphony No. 5. We had a grand total of one afternoon rehearsal (the day before) and one morning rehearsal before the concert that night. Because the ensemble seldom experiences turnover, it plays with the intimacy of a chamber orchestra, which reminded me of how Georg Szell molded the Cleveland Orchestra and got its unique sound. My jazz friends call it "tight."

Yehudi Menuhin was the Varsovia's music director, although he performed only a few concerts a year with them. At one point in the rehearsal of the Beethoven Fifth I suggested to the string players some bowings different from those they had penciled in their parts. My idea for the second movement was to stagger the bowings so that some of the players would be playing upward with the bow while others would be going downward. I wanted to force a continuous sound in order to achieve longer phrases. As I was giving my suggestions the concertmaster asked if he could speak to me for a few minutes. In a quiet, modest, but somewhat pleading voice he said, "Lord Menuhin always thinks he understands orchestral bowings even though his seldom work. He is a great violin soloist but his ideas have no bearing on preparing proper orchestral bowings. We're going to be performing the same piece with him next month and he'll have a fit if he sees someone else's bowings. If you'll agree not to change them we'll do everything possible to make the phrases as long as you want." I agreed and was reminded of an important lesson. Because of my work with George Zazofsky, I *thought* I knew better than the concertmaster how best to achieve my wishes. Fred Prausnitz once told me it is always best to leave bowing decisions to the principal strings, even if you can pick up the violin and play it as well or better than the concertmaster. Fred gets smarter every year.

This particular concert fell on the fiftieth anniversary of Hitler's death and there had been threats throughout Germany of skinhead demonstrations. So there I was, a Jewish conductor leading a Polish orchestra in a performance of Beethoven's Fifth. I considered doing it in double time so I could get out of there lickety-split. Of course, that would have been impossible and in the end all went well. And I didn't encounter any demonstrators.

Once I accepted an invitation to conduct an orchestra about which I knew nothing. Big mistake. When I arrived in the second largest city in Slovakia everything seemed nice enough, and I was especially pleased when the driver who took me to the hotel paid me the total fee in advance. It seems that the person usually responsible for payment was out of the city until the following weekend.

The Košice State Philharmonic of Slovakia was mediocre at best and not eager to work. I pushed the musicians hard during the first rehearsal, even harder during the second. At the break during the third rehearsal the manager said he wanted to speak to me because things apparently weren't going well. I told him I couldn't agree more. Little progress had been made, and I suggested that we speak immediately. We went to his office, where I met the violin soloist, who happened to be an assistant to

Dorothy DeLay, the famous teacher and a good friend of mine. The manager told me that the orchestra was not happy with my work method, that I was too demanding, and couldn't I lighten up? I was furious, not to any small degree because he was saying this in front of the soloist. I lost it and told him what I thought in a loud voice. Those who know me think of me as soft-spoken—but I wasn't, not on that day, not in that office. By the time I finished my unprepared speech I was screaming. When he asked what I suggested we do I said, "I think it best that I leave this afternoon, and you can tell people you fired me if you want. Just change the airplane ticket while I wait." He became more than a bit nervous and said that would mean paying a penalty for changing the flight. When I pointed out that the extra expense would be offset by a considerably lower hotel bill, he accepted my proposal.

I instructed him to have the driver come to the hotel to take me to the airport in two hours. I left happily, went directly to a bank, exchanged currency from the paycheck they had given me, and awaited the driver. About halfway to the airport the driver asked politely if I would be willing to return part of the fee, because the manager hadn't known that it had been given to me before the time of my "firing." I turned to her and laughed. So did she.

There was one orchestra that never invited me to conduct. A distant cousin, Theodore Bloomfield, was for a number of years music director of the Sinfonie Orchester Berlin. On two occasions I made contact with Teddy, once personally and the other through a German management, to see if there might be a possibility of my guest conducting that orchestra. Both replies were the same. No, because he was worried about inviting Americans, especially if they were Jewish, and even more especially if they were in any way related. I was disappointed, but I did have a good laugh when I saw at the top of the orchestra's letterhead in large and bold print the letters "SOB."

The most interesting forty-eight hours I ever spent in musical travels happened during my third guest-conducting venture in Ostrava, a fairly large industrial city now in the Czech Republic. For reasons I don't recall, there was a day that week without rehearsals. I asked for and received permission to do two things, one of which was to speak to a few students, with no professors present, at the conservatory after my rehearsal, something I often do. My experience has been that students everywhere feel freer to express their opinions in a closed session. I also asked for a twenty-four-hour visa to take a train to Kraków, Poland, where I'd not previously been and which is just across their border.

When I was ushered into what I thought would be a small classroom I found myself in an auditorium, facing faculty sitting together on the left and students on the right. I quickly realized that they expected some type of speech, and since I had nothing prepared, I immediately launched into something about how fortunate they were to live in a country that provided funds for the arts, something that was not common in my country, blah, blah. All this I did through my translator. What I hadn't in the least expected was the blasting I took from the faculty about decadent American composers and the false hype that surrounds such schools as Juilliard and the Curtis Institute. They also extolled the glories of communism that encourage "forward-looking" artists. After about twenty minutes I realized that none of the students was going to be allowed to speak, even when I addressed questions to that side of the room. So I told everyone there that I had hoped only to spend an hour or so with a few students, and that I was not there to defend my country against verbal attacks: "See ya later, alligator." I'm not sure how that translated.

Then I went with the orchestra manager to the Polish Consulate to obtain the visa and left on the train for Kraków. I had been given a map of the city and decided to set out on foot in an attempt to discover why it has been considered such an artistic gem for centuries. Since the famous Frederic Chopin Conservatory was not on the map, I tried to ask two nuns to tell me how to get there. "Where is the . . ." was all I got out before they actually ran from me. The American devil had arrived, at least in their minds. Next I saw two youngsters shooting basketball. I motioned that I'd like to join them, they agreed, and were somewhat amazed that a forty-something foreigner could still drill it.

Afterward I went to a small café; after I'd been there a while I saw some students all dressed up and carrying musical instruments. I paid my bill and followed them. They were going to the conservatory for an afternoon concert. I tagged along and heard a sixteen-year-old give an astounding rendition of the Paganini Violin Concerto No. 1. I talked to his teacher (in English) afterward to see if the young man might be interested in attending EMF if a scholarship could be arranged, and I headed back to the train station for the return to Ostrava. Then the real fun began.

I knew that the name of the train was the Chopin Express, but there were no signs distinguishing one train from the other, and no one inside at the ticket booth spoke English. Because I wasn't able to say "Chopin" in such a manner that made me understandable, I began to get very nervous. If I got on the wrong train not only would I miss the next morning's rehearsal, but also my visa would expire. I was frustrated but finally decided to jump aboard what seemed to be the least grimy and longest train (the Chopin Express still travels through four countries) just as it was leaving the station.

I was in a state of panic trying to get the train conductor to speak to me or at least look at my ticket, when who should appear but Ms. Santa Claus. Actually, I don't recall her name but when she said, "Don't worry, this is the train that stops in Ostrava," she got an unsolicited hug that almost broke her back. She told me that she was a graduate student from Michigan State University doing research in Poland. She also told me she had a few free days and would like to stay in Ostrava to hear the dress rehearsal and concert the following day. After getting off the train we went to the hotel where I was staying to see if they had a vacancy. No problem.

As a way of thanking her, I asked if I could treat her to dinner that evening. At dinner that night in the hotel restaurant we were seated next to three young people, two British women and a German man, who were traveling with what I think was a very minor league circus. They invited Ms. Claus and me to join them, and when we had finished, one of the Brits suggested that we all go to her room. At that point the German said, "Goodie. Groupy sexy." Claus and I declined, but I do think about her every Christmas.

Ostrava has a fine symphony orchestra. They also have a dreadfully uncomfortable concert hall, but the music was so important to their citizens that each time I conducted there the concerts were SRO. I was also encouraged to see so many youngish concertgoers come backstage after the concerts. The person assigned as my guide and translator was a fascinating woman named Alena Veliminska. Her story is a sad one, not unlike many I heard in eastern Europe during those years. Her husband,

George, was a fine surgeon and chief of physicians at the Ostrava Hospital, but his political opinions caused him to be considered a threat to the government, especially after he signed a protest document just before Prague Spring, the famous uprising in 1968. Somehow he escaped imprisonment but was forced to go to work at another hospital about two hundred miles distant; he had permission to return home to see his wife and children but one weekend every two months. George has since died, but Alena, her children, and I stay in touch. She and her daughter Olga visited me in Geneva for five days in 1993, and Alena has done quite well working as a translator in English, French, and German in her hometown.

Near Ostrava there is a small village with a very well-preserved Beethoven House, where he worked on his Symphony No. 4 while in the employ of a wealthy patron. Alena took me there one afternoon and told me that some hundred and fifty or so years earlier Beethoven's patron had said to him something like, "Tonight we have other royalty coming for a big shindig, and I want you to play a recital after dinner." Beethoven said, "No." The patron said, "If you want to stay here, you'll do it." Beethoven said, "Okay." But when recital time came Beethoven, who clearly was a master at infuriating almost everyone he came in contact with, was nowhere to be found. He had hired a coachman to take him back to Vienna. Bravo. He'll always be my main man.

In February 1976 I went to Sarajevo to conduct two concerts, one in that city and a repeat in nearby Banja Luka. I was somewhat surprised when, five minutes into the first rehearsal, the principal cellist challenged me about a rhythm. When I insisted that he do it my way, he simply packed up his cello and left! During the break, while drinking the strongest coffee known to man, I asked the manager whether I should plan to see the cellist during the remainder of rehearsal. He replied that I shouldn't worry, that the man simply hated rehearsals and might or might not return.

Through my translator I had several discussions with various members of the orchestra about the future of their country, and they were unanimous in their prophetic response: "When Tito dies this whole area will blow up." I kept up correspondence with a few of the friends I made while there—until their prophecy became a reality.

The Sarajevo concert went well and when the manager told me that I was to ride in his auto to Banja Luka for the repeat, I told him that I preferred to travel on the train with the orchestra members. When it was time for the train to depart, it didn't. And it was very cold. I was told that the heat would come on when the train actually departed. When the train finally left the station, some ninety minutes late, there still was no heat. A few minutes later the orchestra personnel manager came around with bottles of wine for everyone and said that the wine would make us feel warm.

After the concert the orchestra took the train back to Sarajevo, but I stayed for a reception and dinner being held in my honor. We ate and ate. Then the mayor, who was sitting beside me, proposed a toast and gave me a Yugoslavian hunting knife in a small case. It seemed only appropriate that I open it. We all know that sinking feeling when we cut ourselves and know that the gush of blood is but seconds away. I had sliced the palm of my left hand with the knife, but I didn't want to seem ungrateful or to cause a commotion, so I pretended nothing had happened, all the while wiping the blood on my pants for the next hour or so. Everyone kept eating and the food kept coming. The waiters seemed like robots walking back and forth from the kitchen to the dining area. The meal and reception lasted until well after midnight.

I remember Sarajevo as a beautiful city with a great deal of smog, which I was told was caused by British, Canadian, and United States factories. Furthermore, those same countries had built a new hospital, essentially as a gift for the people who had become sick from the smog. Somehow the rationale escaped me, especially when, after one of the rehearsals, the manager took me for lunch to a fine restaurant in the mountains that overlook the city. Because of the haze, we couldn't see Sarajevo.

In 1983 I conducted the Irish National Radio Orchestra in Dublin in a broadcast that included the Mahler Symphony No. 1. The orchestra had three staff conductors, none of whom suited the musicians. Just before my arrival they had somehow managed to have all three fired or put on notice. They were feeling their oats. Any conductor was now fair game, and it just happened to be me in this instance, although I didn't discover the politics involved until after the broadcast.

Mahler's instructions near the end of the symphony are for the eight horn players to stand with the bells of their instruments facing upward, which creates a marvelous visual and musical effect. At the beginning of the first rehearsal the manager introduced me to the orchestra. I said, "Good morning," and the principal horn player immediately stood up and said, "We're not going to stand at the end of the symphony."

Things went downhill from there. At each rehearsal they would stick to what I wanted and then revert to something different when we did a play through. Even the soloist, who was the principal cellist of the orchestra, had an attitude. When she and I had our private session I told her my philosophy about doing essentially what the soloist wanted unless there was serious disagreement. She responded, "Fine, because that's the way it's going to be whether you like it or not."

By the time of the live broadcast I was furious, and when the orchestra deliberately played a phrase in the slow movement in almost exactly the opposite way we had rehearsed I actually stopped conducting, but they kept playing. Right away the man in the broadcast booth turned on his flashing red lights, waved his arms, and jumped up and down in a panic. So I started again, and as we neared the end of the Mahler I gave my fiercest stare at the horn section, daring them not to stand and put their bells in the air. All in all it was a good stare, but it didn't make any difference. The next morning I went for a walk in a park just outside Dublin and a very dapperly dressed man actually said to me, "Top o' the mornin' to ya." Really. It *almost* made up for the bad performance.

In 1993 I encountered the Russian Mafia when I drove to Gdańsk, Poland, to conduct a concert. I had been warned about car theft by Mariusz Stowpiec, my Polish manager, who insisted that my contract include "Guarded Parking" at the residence, a special apartment building for artists. When I arrived I made certain the gate and auto were locked. I took my briefcase, which held my music, up five flights of stairs to the apartment. I returned to get the rest of the luggage.

When I got back down to "Guarded Parking," I was astonished to see that my automobile had vanished. Where did it go—and so quickly? At that time the Polish police had no computers and the auto was long gone. There is a video that shows Russian Mafia–trained young Poles at work stealing cars. It takes them less than thirty minutes to break the gate, dismantle even the most sophisticated alarm, open the car door, drive it to a warehouse, change the plates and the chassis number, spray-paint it, and place it on a boat destined for Moscow, St. Petersburg, wherever the consignment has been made. Of course I felt violated, but putting the matter into perspective, suppose I had surprised them? Better to lose my clothes and my car than my life.

Besides, I had car insurance—I thought. Weeks later I learned that my Swiss insurance covered only one-half of the value of the auto, since it was stolen outside Switzerland. Of course, according to the Swiss, nobody would steal a car *inside* their country.

At rehearsal the next morning the manager told the orchestra what had happened, and I explained that until I could buy new clothes they might be seeing me in the same outfit—I was wearing jeans—for a few days. At that point the principal clarinetist stood up and said in perfect English, "If I had a pair of stone-washed Levi's I'd wear them 365 days a year." The whole orchestra cracked up. The manager lent me a frock from the opera house for the concert, and by then I had replaced some of my other clothes.

After that concert I went by plane to the next Polish city and another orchestra. As was the case in Gdańsk, the orchestra manager found me a frock at the opera house. While I was dressing for the concert I realized I'd been given two left shoes and it was too late to exchange them. Standing, walking, or conducting for about eighty minutes on two left shoes is as awkward as trying to eat cheese fondue with chopsticks.

In 1996 I was to do a concert in Germany. My wife, Patsy, and I picked up our clothes from the dry cleaners in Geneva and, without checking the hangers, packed for the trip. About an hour before the concert we ripped off the plastic and laid my frock coat and trousers on the bed. The trousers weren't mine—they were Patsy's black slacks, which the cleaners in Geneva had accidentally switched. Somehow, with the assistance of various paper clips and safety pins, we managed to squeeze me into her black pants. After the concert the music director of the orchestra came backstage to congratulate me, and he did mention that my pants looked about five inches too short. When we told him what had happened he simply said, "Oh, I thought perhaps that was a new American style."

During the communist era each eastern European country had special shops for products from the West, especially spirits, perfumes, and cigarettes. But they could be purchased only with "hard" currency. Of course, the kicker was that their citizens were not allowed to have deutsche marks, U.S. dollars, or Swiss or French francs. It was painful to watch the locals peering into these state-owned stores, knowing that for them even to enter, much less try to purchase any goods, could bring severe police penalties.

Once I was invited to do Orff's *Carmina Burana* in Santo Domingo. The orchestra's driver took me from the airport to a luxury hotel that had a huge outdoor swimming pool with a bar in the middle. As I was driven to the rehearsal the next morning, I saw horrible squalor and poverty in every direction, old men sitting in front of their shacks with whisky bottles in hand, naked children staring into space. It was hard to concentrate during rehearsal with those scenes fresh in my mind. The orchestra was not very good, but the chorus sang in a beautifully soulful way. And the auditorium was packed the night of the concert. The people wanted art.

◘ THERE IS A SCENE NEAR THE BEGINNING OF THE FILM *Meeting Venus* to which I can easily relate. A Hungarian conductor is preparing for rehearsals with the Paris Opéra. At his first meeting with the gathering of international singers, he attempts to give a pep talk using his heavily accented English. Quickly discovering that most of the cast has no idea what he is saying, he silently composes the opening line of a letter to his wife: "Only a conductor can be misunderstood simultaneously in eight languages." My French is only somewhat workable, my Spanish and German much worse. But I know restaurant language and had a good time using it and my knowledge of local customs in those years after my mother's death when my father, Irwin, traveled to Europe with me.

He had become my steadfast supporter, and in the last few years of his life we often traveled together when I was guest conducting in Cannes, Aix, Geneva, Budapest (his favorite city), Frankfurt, Seville, and London. I treasure those times because we got to know one another in ways not previously possible. He loved talking about his life before and just after I was born, about his sports ambitions, his friends from high school and the shenanigans they played, the fact that he decided not to continue after one year in college so his brother could go to medical school, and his feelings about various family members. I think he needed someone to listen to him tell his life story—and who better than his oldest son?

When we first went to Spain I warned my father about the dining hours and told him that I'd made reservations at my favorite restaurant in Seville, Maison Don Raimundo, for 10 P.M., when it opened. By 7:30 Irwin had finished the salami I had bought to tide him over, and he insisted, "There must be someplace to go just to get a sandwich." When it got to be 8:30 P.M. and I still hadn't convinced him that there were no restaurants open at that hour, it seemed a good idea to go for a walk and show him the posted hours on the restaurants' entrances. When it finally got to be ten o'clock I thought he was going to break down the door at Don Raimundo's. We were the first ones there, and he had finished all he could eat before the next customers arrived. The following day he went to a supermarket and bought about ten bags of chips, all the packaged meat he could find, and several bottles of wine. For the remainder of that week his hotel room looked like a set from *The Beverly Hillbillies*.

I always had the situation under control in terms of foreign languages and customs when Irwin traveled with me, but I was concerned on one trip when we went to Budapest. Our first night there was not a problem, since we ate in the hotel restaurant, using menus that were translated into English—somewhat. He got a big kick out of their wine list, which announced, "Please to try our wines. They will leave you nothing to hope for." The manager of the opera orchestra that I was to conduct suggested another place for dinner our second evening. We went in, and I knew right away that I was in major trouble with the language, so I decided just to wing it. When the waiter came over to our table I looked up and said something like, "Grinshin plzitce lutshaba burtch kikia lasco hishkin. Tak?" The poor man just looked at me, gave a shrug, and came back with several plates of delicious Hungarian food. Irwin looked at me, somewhat awestruck, and said, "I'm really impressed. I never knew you could speak Hungarian too." Only when we returned to the States did I tell him the truth. He loved it and told the story to anyone who would listen.

What a wonderful way for us to become really good friends. He was also my best musical critic, never hesitating to make suggestions after rehearsals. My one regret is that he was of the old world and never found it possible (even on his deathbed) to say, "I love you." He went into a hospital in Greensboro on a Friday afternoon. I awoke the following Sunday shortly after midnight, somehow knowing something was wrong, and drove to his hospital only to find that he had been moved to intensive care. I raced there just before he lost consciousness, in time to see him raise his right hand over the bed rail and give me a thumbs up sign—and a smile. Less than an hour later he was dead. And I was an orphan.

THIRTEEN

Players Out of Tune

BEING A SUCCESSFUL EXECUTIVE DIRECTOR (THEY USED TO be called orchestra managers) in today's cloudy artistic climate is a great task. It should go without saying, but doesn't, that a director must have a love for the art form. Also, he or she should be able to direct the staff in a steady and caring manner, deal with ever-changing board chairs and members, be personable with all the concert-going public and the musicians, oversee the increasingly difficult attempts at fund-raising, and work closely with the music director in myriad ways. Perhaps most important, the good executive director must be honorable: open, respectful of differing views, and honest at all times.

It is not surprising that executive directors change jobs so frequently, and not necessarily because they are competent. I know of one whose orchestra went bankrupt, just as did his next one, and the one after that. And this man is still in the business. Could all three boards have been that bad? I doubt it.

Another one decided to save money on an outdoor concert by keeping the piano onstage between the rehearsal and the performance. He ended up paying a hundred times the cost of moving the instrument when an unexpected thunderstorm destroyed it. This same manager scheduled a concert in a nearby town but forgot to put it on the orchestra schedule. The only people who showed up were the soloist (who had to be paid) and the audience. When he applied for his present job, nobody on the search committee thought to call his previous employer.

Executive directors are an interesting breed, regardless of the level of the orchestra. In 1985 I was invited to give a lecture to students who were master's degree candidates at the State University of New York at Binghamton music school's artist management course. During the question-and-answer period I posed the following question: "Would you prefer to manage an orchestra in North America if you had an alternative offer of a position in a country where you wouldn't have to be concerned with fund-raising?" The first response was, "I'm only interested in how fast I can put a BMW in my garage." With one exception, the others agreed. They had no interest in helping an organization produce quality art.

I've known a few managers who have been absolutely first-class, but they are certainly not the norm. Sy Rosen held such positions as manager of the Pittsburgh Symphony Orchestra and the Philadelphia Orchestra, director of Carnegie Hall, and dean of the Arizona State University School of Music. Another who comes to mind is Joan Brichetti, who "made" the Richmond Symphony before moving on to the St. Louis Symphony; she played a great role helping that orchestra move into the upper echelon of North American ensembles. Jackie Taylor, an EMF alum, is now doing fine work as executive director of Chamber Music at Lincoln Center. John Edwards, the executive director of the Chicago Symphony for many years, once said, "Any orchestra that ends their season with a surplus is doing something wrong." Edwards was one of the great executive directors, and I am certain he wasn't advocating large deficits, just trying to send a message to those who have so much control over the North American musical world.

EMF has had a series of executive directors, ranging from excellent to ridiculous. Jim Newlin, whom I mentioned earlier as the Guilford College administrator who, with the help of some students, raised enough money to save EMF, was exemplary. At the other extreme was a man who held the position for nearly three years and always referred to the organization as EFM, regardless of the hundreds of times he was corrected. I sometimes worried that he was going to address a soloist last name first, as in, "Wasn't Ma Yo-Yo really wonderful last night?" Incidentally, he came to EMF from International Concert Management (ICM), one of the largest artist management agencies in the United States.

When conductors are forced out of their positions, it is usually due to behind-the-scenes collaboration between the executive director and the board. I was not immune to such an attempt. In 1989–90 I faced the most difficult time of my professional life because of the dishonesty and manipulations of EMF's executive director, Walter Heid.

In January 1989 a very frightened EMF office manager told me that Heid had been doctoring the budgets for several years to make it appear that the Festival was always in the black. The materials she showed me appeared to be evidence of fraud. For example, she showed me thank-you letters to three national foundations. Each donation had been designated for scholarships, and each letter listed the recipient and the amount of the scholarship awarded. The problem was that many students were listed several times. For example, Joe Blatz was listed in *each* letter as having received a scholarship award of $2,000 for a total of $6,000—this at a time when total tuition and all other fees were $2,800. Neither she nor I knew where the remaining $3,200 was appearing, although our guess was that it was being added to a general fund-raising line item that would make Walter look good in the eyes of the board. Wherever the money went, it was obvious to me that something was definitely wrong.

I took the information to the board treasurer and asked him to deal with it. I explained that I wanted no further involvement, nor did the office manager, who feared for her job. The treasurer studied the photocopies of the letters for a few minutes and said, "I'm going to set up a meeting with the board president as soon as possible to get to the bottom of this. Don't worry."

A few months later I returned from guest conducting in Europe to find that my presence was requested at a "Blue Ribbon Committee" meeting. When I asked the purpose of the meeting I was told that the committee had been established to deal with me and the manner in which I had been doing my job. I telephoned Joe Bryan, Jr., who advised me to get an attorney right away. I engaged Scott Gayle, who became a very special friend and later joined the EMF board. We began preparing our defense by confronting the inevitable question—defense against what?

The charges made against me at the meeting were absurd. I was accused of trying to get the executive director in trouble with the current board and causing instability within the organization. For years I had written "letters to the file" about all my professional dealings. At my meeting with the committee I brought several dozen files that easily refuted all their accusations—I thought. When the meeting was over Scott said to me, "That wasn't a trial, that was a witch hunt."

One week after the meeting, the committee found me guilty of both charges, and I received a "findings" report. The new board president gave me something close to marching orders. He told me privately, "If you expect to continue as music director you are not to have any dealings with any staff or board members. Also, if possible, I strongly suggest that you consider moving." He was actually reading from a prepared script, and he watched me write each word he said on napkins.

I followed his suggestion, sold my house, and moved—probably a good deal farther away than he expected. My choice was Geneva, Switzerland. I had many friends from my concerts there over the years, I had always loved the city, and the location was perfect as a base from which to travel to conduct other concerts throughout Europe.

Two years later I was guest conducting in Warsaw. After a rehearsal I returned to the hotel and was given a fax sent from the new board president of EMF, Gerald Truesdale. Walter Heid had been fired, the festival's debt was enormous, the endowment had been raided. Gerald's fax ended, "Please tell me what to do now." I couldn't get to a typewriter fast enough.

By the following year all but one of the fifteen members of that Blue Ribbon Committee had apologized for their actions.

My suggestion to board chairs and members is to be astutely aware of the organization's operations, but, unless there is an imperative reason to do otherwise, shut up and let music directors and executive directors get their work done. My suggestion to executive directors is to believe fervently in the organization and always be meticulous and completely aboveboard in financial dealings. My suggestion to music directors is to spend more time studying and less time reworking their résumés. Most

North American orchestras experience turmoil from time to time at least in part because the board, executive directors, or music directors are doing something other than what is best for the organization.

◧ ONE AFTERNOON IN THE BEAU-RIVAGE PALACE, A SUMP-tuous hotel in Lausanne, Switzerland, I met with the renowned Polish composer Krzysztof Penderecki and his elegant wife, Elisabeth, to discuss the possibility of his coming to EMF. Somehow we got on the subject of artists' managers and how incompetent, arrogant, greedy, and insensitive most of them are. And those were the repeatable words, his English is that good. "Down with the lot of them," Penderecki concluded, proposing a toast. I raised my goblet of Perrier, clinked it against his, and broke my glass. As the liveried waiters rushed from all corners of the room to mop up the mess and I tried to find enough ways to apologize, his wife, ever the diplomat, said, "Now *that* is a proper Polish toast. Bravo, Maestro!"

Most solo artists' managers are as slippery as bad used-car salesmen and see us musicians as flesh to be peddled for the most dollars the market will bear. I have dealt with artists' managers who tried to "sell" me an artist they had never met or even heard perform. A few years ago I foolishly engaged a soprano on a manager's recommendation and because the cassette he sent me of her was overwhelmingly gorgeous. When she opened her mouth at rehearsal and sang the first note, horribly off-key, my heart sank. *She wasn't the same person I'd heard on the tape!*

The majority of artists' managers in North America require that an artist pay a sizable monthly retainer in addition to footing the bill for publicity materials, photos, mailings, and phone calls—without any guarantee of bookings. And this is in addition to the 15–20 percent the manager takes from all fees. The 1999 annual directory *Musical America* lists nearly five hundred North American management agencies. Of the artists' managers I've dealt with in my career, I can count a grand total of four whom I consider honorable. I finally stopped dealing with artist management firms when I realized almost all my conducting engagements were coming by word of mouth.

My last personal manager, Mariusz Stopiec, was educated in Warsaw and then the London School of Economics. After his return to Warsaw he worked for the official state artist management agency, PAGART. However, Mariusz foresaw the downfall of communism, and when the Berlin Wall came down he was ready to go. He had already rented office space for his new firm, ARISTA, and had secured financing from Elisabeth Penderecki. A more decent, humorous, and visionary man I've never known. Mariusz deeply cared about music and musicians. We became good friends.

ARISTA signed me to a contract that called for two concerts each season in Poland, the country of my grandparents. One evening Mariusz invited my wife and me to a traditional dinner at his home in Warsaw. We soon discovered that a traditional Polish dinner consists mostly of one shot of vodka after another, although his wife did serve food from time to time as a sort of side dish. We watched as Dorota and Mariusz drank more than one bottle each—we had quit much earlier. When the evening came to a close he somehow staggered around outside and found us a taxi. When he arrived at the hotel the next morning to take us to the airport he said that he had devoured ten aspirin and felt fine, which is the only lie he ever told me.

A few weeks later I was back in Geneva and received a phone call from a mutual friend. Mariusz had been killed, stabbed by a student of his wife. I faxed for confirmation. True. And tragic.

At the other end of the artistic manager spectrum was Ron Wilford, president of Columbia Artists Management, Incorporated (CAMI), the most powerful management agency worldwide. He was as cold and disagreeable as Mariusz was caring and encouraging. In 1973 I had a meeting with him that Marvin Schofer, then Wilford's associate and someone I highly respect, had arranged. I told Ron that while I had enjoyed my guest-conducting experiences in Europe, I wanted more guest-conducting opportunities in North America. He replied, "I'm managing eighty conductors, most of whom would love to have your schedule." After I responded that my concern was not about the other conductors he replied, "There really isn't anything else I can do for you, but please know that my door is always open. Sorry, but I have to go to another meeting." With that he got up and left me sitting in an important leather

138

chair in front of his desk. And as a silly symbolic gesture, he exited without closing the door—or shaking my hand, for that matter.

◙ THE PERSON I CONSIDER THE FINEST AMERICAN-BORN and -trained performer on any instrument was, to my mind, the violinist Michael Rabin. He had such total and absolute control over the instrument that even as a teenager he never once had to look at the fingerboard to see where to place his left-hand fingers. Michael's manager, CAMI, was only too pleased to be able to brag in his LP liner notes and his official bio that he had already traveled tens of thousands of miles as a soloist by the time he was sixteen. It was a brutal schedule that no teenager—or adult—could sustain.

Michael came twice to EMF, the first time after his second nervous breakdown. When the festival re-engaged him in 1970 he asked if he could stay in a hotel the night of his concerto. I thought the request a bit strange because he had previously seemed to love his interaction with the students, especially after his performances. That night he looked woozy to me backstage and even while we were performing. After the concert we were headed to my car to go to a reception at the home of Leah Tannenbaum, then the board president, when Michael fell on the pavement. With some help from a faculty member, the pianist Warren Rich, we were able to get him to Leah's. Her husband, Jack, was a doctor and I quickly told him what had happened. He immediately asked to see Michael's violin. When Jack opened the case and found various drugs he said, "Take Rabin back and get rid of those drugs. If he takes any more tonight he'll die." Warren went back with us to the hotel, and by then the drugs were beginning to wear off. Michael walked up to the hotel desk clerk and said, "These guys are trying to hurt me. Please stop them from going to my room." We had no choice but to leave. When I telephoned his room at seven the next morning he had already checked out.

A few months later I saw Michael in New York City, where I was living, and he acted as though nothing out of the ordinary had happened at EMF. We joked a bit and made plans to have lunch soon afterward. But the lunch never happened. He committed suicide in January of the following year. The official autopsy report makes specific mention of large doses of barbiturates in his body.

Soon after his death I received a telephone call from a pianist I had never met. He was a friend of both Warren Rich and Michael, and he asked if we could meet for a few minutes. I don't remember his name because it has been about thirty years, and I never saw him again. To my knowledge the high point of his career was playing the first movement of the Grieg Piano Concerto with the Boston Pops—or so he told me. More important, he also told me that he had been with Michael the night of the overdose and was desperate because he had been told about the episode at EMF and had feared for months that Michael was planning to commit suicide with drugs. He pleaded with me to keep my mouth shut. CAMI was attempting a cover-up, denying that Michael had died from anything other than falling over a chair, although the rumors had already spread. I agreed, "Fine, I won't say anything about last summer." And I've kept my word on that. Until now.

Ten years later a friend of mine wanted to write an article about Michael for *New York Magazine* and asked if I could assist. No problem, since it was to be a tribute to him. Except that everyone who knew the truth was still running scared, especially employees at CAMI. No one was even willing to be interviewed.

The power of artists' management agencies should not be underestimated. Their control over individual artists as well as orchestras and boards shapes much of North America's musical life, often to its detriment.

An example is Seiji Ozawa, who is managed by CAMI. In part because of Wilford's contacts on the board of the Boston Symphony Orchestra (BSO), in part because CAMI manages the orchestra's touring schedule, this conductor of unknown ability was named music director in 1972. Knowledgeable music lovers, onstage and off, thought the BSO deserved better. Some in the hierarchy of the Tanglewood Festival, summer home of the BSO, grumbled that Ozawa doesn't understand its educational mission. In fact, two music directors resigned because of their fundamental curriculum and teaching disagreements with him. But CAMI called the shots and Ozawa played the tunes. In July 1999 Ozawa announced he would step down from his BSO and Tanglewood positions in 2002. As several players told me, most of the orchestra's musicians are apprehensive about who will replace him, although they did breathe a sigh of relief about his impending departure.

FOURTEEN

Where Did All the Melodies Go?

I REMAIN ASTONISHED THAT ALMOST ANY MUSIC WRITTEN IN the twentieth century, especially Bartók's, continues to strike fear into so many North American concertgoers. "Can't we just stick to the standards and forget about Stravinsky, Hindemith, and especially that blasted Bartók?"

Where did all our post-Bartók classical music composers go? In the last half of the twentieth century, pretty much nowhere, writing lots of nonsense and using gimmicks that are increasingly driving people *away* from our concert halls. In North America we had Leonard Bernstein, who wrote one quality composition for theater, *West Side Story*, and Aaron Copland, whose Symphony No. 3 is in my opinion great music. What we have now are lots of mediocre compositions by mediocre composers in search of something that escapes me and most of my fellow musicians worldwide. For example, who would go to a performance of John Cage's *Atlas Eclipticalis*, or of the piece he wrote for fifty-two harpsichords, which takes four hours to perform, the title of which I have blissfully forgotten? Or what about Morton Subotnick's *Play No. 2*, which

David Daniels describes in his *Orchestral Music* as having "graph" music? Some pseudo-intellectuals, critics, and curiosity seekers might attend performances of these, but I can't imagine they'd learn anything or enjoy any of it. Recently I saw an advertisement for a program that included *Music for Five Percussion Ensembles and Strings* and *Weather Rhythms*. In the advertisement the composers weren't even identified! I wonder if the sponsors thought leaving the composers' names off the posters would attract a larger audience.

In the 1970s the Chinese government decided to commission a composition for piano soloist and orchestra to be titled *The Yellow River Concerto*. The commission was awarded to a group of Chinese composers who, by some sort of consensus, decided which notes to include and where. The piece was then recorded by the young American pianist Daniel Epstein, whose manager (as well as the recording company) thought it would "make" his career and lots of money for the producers. It was grade-D film music at best, but lots of copies were sold before the critics had time to pan it. The reason I know this? I bought it. Even I can be conned.

Early in this century Germany and Austria gave us Berg, Hindemith, Mahler, and Richard Strauss; from Russia we had Prokofiev, Rachmaninoff, Scriabin, Shostakovich, and Stravinsky; France produced Debussy, Fauré, Milhaud, Ravel, and Saint-Saëns. And of course there's that blasted Bartók from Hungary. All these great composers wrote pieces that are staples of today's repertoire. However, most other composers after Mahler and Bartók decided to strike out in different directions, not only using electronic devices but also playing traditional instruments in ways not taught in our music schools.

In 1976 I conducted a broadcast performance of György Ligeti's Cello Concerto in Hilversum, the Netherlands. I had no choice in the program, and would have preferred nearly any other composition. The opening is so slow that the conductor is instructed to move the baton only every ten seconds. To make matters worse, by the time less than three minutes have gone by the soloist is playing fifteen notes per beat, the first violins are playing thirteen notes per beat, the second violins twelve notes per beat, and the violas ten notes per beat. It is totally absurd and literally impossible to realize. However, I did mention the per-

143

formance to the late cellist Roger Drinkall, who was scheduled to do a concerto with me at EMF the following year. Roger was quite excited and asked if we could do the Ligeti. Probably because I had gone to such effort to learn it I agreed.

At that time the EPO concertmaster was Harold Wolf, an extraordinary violinist of the old school. Harold is one of those rare musicians who love the classics; when being told that something like the Tchaikovsky Fifth Symphony is being programmed, he reacts with glee even though he has played it hundreds of times before. When the Ligeti rehearsal time came and we arrived at the multitude of rhythms, Harold said to no one in particular, "Fuck it. I ain't playing this shit." And with that, he got up and started to walk out. Most orchestra members, who clearly agreed with Harold, gave him a boisterous round of applause. It took a great deal of persuasion to get him to return.

I suspect post-Mahler composers were, for the most part, intimidated by the search for "How do I top that?"—the same intimidation that Brahms felt before he was able to write his Symphony No. 1, knowing it would be compared to Beethoven's Ninth. In fact, Brahms was so overwhelmed by the thought of the inevitable comparison that the first symphony he attempted ended up as his Piano Concerto No. 1, in which, as a pianist, he had more confidence. Nonetheless, he was able to build on Beethoven and other predecessors and create many great works.

Unfortunately, many of the composers who followed Mahler ignored him and followed Schoenberg's twelve-tone row with all its restrictions, including the demand that each of the twelve notes in a given scale be played before any can be repeated. It seems to me that the Schoenberg cult was forced to try to make music out of mathematical equations. On the other hand, 150 years earlier Mozart wrote a twelve-tone row (with the exception of one grace note) in the first movement of his Symphony No. 40.

The United States has had composers such as Samuel Barber, Karel Husa, and Gunther Schuller, who have written good and important works, but the majority of the repertoire of the last seventy-five years consists of little more than either music written for pure entertainment— for the purpose of receiving additional commissions— or compositions that experiment with atonalities that are intended not to stir but to shock.

Joe Thayer, the dean of the Colburn School of the Performing Arts in Los Angeles, told me he once was assigned to write a paper, "The Essence of Walter Piston's Music," in his final semester. Having already done well in the class, Joe turned in a handful of blank pages. His teacher gave him an F on the "essay." I would have given him an A+.

Actually, there is one composition, *The Baroque Variations*, written by my friend Lukas Foss, that I suspect (I never had the nerve to ask) was written tongue-in-cheek and includes amusing options. The musicians can choose to play—or not—in specific passages, purposely bow *above* the strings so as *not* to produce sound, and throw bass or snare drum sticks from one side of the stage to the other. When I performed it at EMF we used frisbees—I was worried that a snare drum stick might accidently hit one of the woodwind players. The audience loved it, but that sort of thing works only once.

Like many of my colleagues I have done much to further the cause of contemporary composers, European as well as North American, usually out of a sense of obligation, even when I dislike the sounds. By doing this we music directors have driven away some of our audience. This is not to say that there is no audience for even the most avant-garde classical music.

At the Eastern Music Festival we inaugurated a weekly series named for and based on a series in Geneva called "Musique et Sandwich." There the ticket price includes a sandwich to eat while listening, but you have to pay for the coffee—the Swiss think of everything when money is involved. At EMF the concert was free but you had to pay for all of your lunch. The one ground rule for our "Music and Sandwich" was that only music written in the last fifty years could be performed. The audience grew to about seventy-five faithful plus some youngsters from EMF. I view these programs as having educational value for our students. Likewise, our students and audience learned from the festival's Native American Week, which featured a performance and lecture/demonstrations by a contemporary American Indian classical composer. Since the venues for these programs were not "main stage," they did not affect appreciably our audience numbers.

Wynton Marsalis is often criticized for not taking jazz forward but rather attempting to get back to its roots. Despite his critics, Wynton recently won a Pulitzer Prize. My suggestion is that there is untapped talent in composers worldwide and that they would do well to do just as Wynton has done: consider the roots before going forward. Wynton is as concerned about the future of jazz as I am about the future of the classical symphony orchestra. Perhaps our classical composers should be relearning something like the Mahler Symphony No. 5 to give them a model from which to develop their own idioms.

The former program director of the NPR station in Chapel Hill once telephoned to tell me that someone I'd probably never heard of, Mark Murphy, was coming to visit him and that he had a cassette he wanted me to hear. Someone I'd probably never heard of? I had been a fan of Mark Murphy since my Northwestern days. Mark, although not African American, was a terrific jazz singer, much along the lines of Joe Williams, and he moved easily in Chicago's music scene, regardless of his skin color. What I heard was a heady arrangement, à la Quincy Jones, of about seventy minutes of the music of Harold Arlen. It was performed by the Netherlands National Radio Orchestra with a few professional jazz musicians for some of the bass, percussion, and trumpet parts; it featured Mark and a female singer from Amsterdam as the vocalists. Arlen wrote songs that even youngish North Americans have heard frequently, such as "Over the Rainbow," "One for My Baby (And One More for the Road)," "That Old Black Magic," "Stormy Weather," and hundreds of other Broadway tunes that jazz musicians love to play. I thought a concert of these pieces would make a lot of Bartók-haters happy and would be an excellent experience for our students, who need to hear good jazz. When I proposed doing "A Tribute to Harold Arlen" the EMF board went wild—until they realized that we would have to pay fees for the singers and the extra jazz musicians. The consensus was that pop or jazz musicians shouldn't expect *that kind of money* for their work.

With few exceptions (Penderecki's *To the Victims of Hiroshima* and *Threnody*, Husa's *Music for Prague 1968*, and Schuller's *Seven Studies on Themes of Paul Klee* come to mind) I am largely ambivalent about anything post-Bartók, post-Stravinsky, post-Hindemith. I'm a reactionary only in musical terms—in part because I don't like what is forced on me by most of today's composers and because I want my granddaughter, now three years old, to be able to attend a live classical music performance in 2005.

146

FIFTEEN

The Superstar Ripoff

WHEN YO-YO MA CAME TO EMF HE WAS A SHY YOUNG MAN who played wonderfully and gave a dreadful master class because he was so timid and his voice was so soft. Time, fame, and a whole lot of money have brought about a sea change in his public persona. Leonard Rose had asked me to engage Yo-Yo early in his career, to give him some public exposure, and I was happy to oblige. Yet when it came time for a payback, Yo-Yo refused. The summer after Leonard died I wanted to honor the man who had been a mentor to me and Yo-Yo with a memorial concert at the festival—at no fee, so we could offer Leonard Rose Memorial Scholarships. Yo-Yo told me that he was no longer performing in the summertime. But that same summer he performed several times at Tanglewood, where I feel certain he got his full fee.

If you look at the roster of soloists for the leading North American orchestras you will usually see the same "superstars" year after year. What chance do other soloists have when orchestras and promoters of concert series are willing to pay fifty thousand dollars and up per night for an Itzhak Perlman, Anne-Sophie Mutter, or Yo-Yo Ma, to say nothing of the Three Tenors, who receive one million dollars for their trio performances? And these are just a few of the examples. My estimate would be that there are about thirty people in this category, and I challenge anyone to find a year, any year, when at least half of them do not appear at least once in New York City.

EMF was asked by the State of North Carolina to be their delegated arts organization to celebrate Israel's Fiftieth Anniversary in 1998. Years earlier I had engaged the young Israeli violinist Shlomo Mintz, that time at the request of Isaac Stern via Leonard Rose. When I asked Schlomo to be part of the Israeli fête not only did he refuse to come for less than twenty thousand dollars (which he considered a benefit fee!), but he also changed the date of his concert, which wreaked havoc with the schedule. By then it was too late to can the performance, which was my wish, and the board decided he was worth it. Although I was not there for the performance, I was told by the EPO members that his playing was technically wonderful but dull, and they had the feeling that it was just another day at the office for him. Not much happened musically.

In 1992 I read a rave review in the *International Herald Tribune (IHT)* of a performance Daniel Barenboim had conducted with the Deutsche Staatsoper Berlin. The article said that although they had paid Barenboim one million deutsche marks (about $650,000 at the time), he was worth it because the production was so wonderful. I was outraged, in part because Barenboim is also music director of the Chicago Symphony, where he conducts about six of their twenty-eight subscription concerts in an average season and receives (I am told) a very healthy seven-figure salary. Nobody in the not-for-profit arts world is worth that kind of money. This review appeared at the time when the Alabama Symphony, the New Orleans Philharmonic, and the San Diego Symphony were declaring bankruptcy, forcing more than 250 orchestral musicians out of work.

For the first time in my life I wrote a letter to the editor of the *IHT*, which the paper published under the title "Subsidies and Superstars." It read as follows:

> In North America, where government subsidies for the arts are
> minuscule, professional performing-arts organizations are declaring

bankruptcy at an alarming rate. In Europe, where subsidies have been cut, along with social programs, some performing-arts organizations are becoming second-rate artistically. Yet Daniel Barenboim accepts one million Deutsche marks for a four-month period with the Berlin Staatsoper. Numerous North American soloists and conductors are cutting back their fees in an attempt to stem the tide of first-class performers who find themselves out of work without warning. Mr. Barenboim would do well to follow the example set by other so-called "superstars."*

I never dreamed they would publish it. I was both horrified and delighted. A week later I was in Paris and ran into my friend Gerard Poulet, perhaps the finest violinist in France these days. Gerard said, "I saw your letter in the *IHT* this morning and absolutely agree with what you wrote." I understand that an outstanding quarterback in the National Football League earns much more than does Barenboim, but the situations have little in common. The NFL is not in danger of going out of business.

Superstars often achieve their status by working with "name" teachers, sometimes being superior performers, having powerful managers, and knowing people in high places, not necessarily in that order. Luck and timing also help. There are many who have tried to achieve superstar status through other means, such as a dazzling technique, but never attained it. In 1978 I engaged the violinist Jamie Buswell to be an artist-in-residence at EMF and to perform Vivaldi's *Four Seasons*. Before rehearsing with the orchestra, we had a piano session to mutually decide on tempi and style. When we finished, everything seemed fine. But at the rehearsal Jamie's tempi were so fast that after a few minutes the EPO concertmaster asked for a word with Jamie and me. "Jamie, I can't even play that fast, to say nothing of the other violinists behind me." I added, "Jamie, I can't even move the baton that quickly." Jamie agreed to slow down, and the rest of the rehearsal went quite well. But in the concert that night he reverted to pyrotechnics, and we barely made it to the end. Standing backstage afterward watching our students pleading for his au-

---

International Herald Tribune, November 13, 1992, 7.

tograph just made me more furious. I was startled when I heard a familiar voice speak softly to me from behind. It was Meyer Maskin, the noted psychiatrist, whose son was our English horn faculty member and who had come from Florida to hear the concert. He whispered, "Why don't you just walk over to Buswell and say thanks? It can't hurt." It didn't, but Jamie was never again engaged to return to the Festival. Irritating music directors is a surefire means of *not* becoming a superstar.

Too many superstars like Ma and Mintz have very short memories and listen too much to their personal managers. And I question the ability of so many in this tiny elite group, which of course includes several conductors, to sustain their performance standards. How can anyone have time to improve or even maintain his or her artistry while performing a hundred or more concerts a year? Everybody needs to practice, everybody needs study time. I wonder if someone like Perlman performs any better than—even as well as—Franco Gulli? Is Ma playing any better today than a dozen other cellists who deserve a solo career? I suspect it depends on which night you hear them. And what of the orchestra members who accompany these people? How does the section violist of a good orchestra feel when he realizes he doesn't earn as much in a year as the superstar gets for one night?

I also wonder why most of these superstars are not willing to take time off to teach in a serious manner. Money? Most of today's superstars pay lip service to education, but they are not really involved in it to any substantial degree. True, there are exceptions. Michael Tree, the violist in the Guarneri String Quartet, somehow manages to play many concerts a year and yet he finds the time to teach at three different music schools. Franco Gulli has a wonderful violin studio at Indiana University and is famous for the master classes he gives worldwide. But the Michaels and Francos won't be with us forever.

SIXTEEN

Movers, Fakers, and Funders

◈

W HEN I WAS LIVING IN BOSTON IN 1965 I HAD A TELE-
phone call from a good friend from high school days who was working
as an administrative assistant in Senator Sam Ervin's Washington office.
He said that the senator had told him that the National Endowment for
the Arts (NEA) was in the process of choosing its directors and he had
taken the liberty of calling Livingston Biddle, Jr., deputy to the first
chairman of the NEA, to ask if he would meet with me to discuss the
position of director of the music division.

Biddle and I hit it off immediately, and we shared ideas all afternoon.
He is one of the few nonartists who honestly care and are passionate
about the well-being of the arts. Biddle told me that the decision was
not totally his, that it had to be approved by an NEA panel at their next
meeting the following month. He said that if I would file a formal application he would send it on with his personal recommendation. He also
assured me that I could have additional "vacation" time, which would
enable me to continue with EMF, and that I wouldn't have to begin the
job until after the 1966 EMF season, about nine months away. What sur-

prised me the most was that Biddle had actually read all the EMF materials my friend had mailed him and that he wanted the NEA music director to be someone who would continue as a practitioner.

I left D.C. feeling good about the meeting and told my wife, Rebecca, that we should start looking for an apartment there. One night about three weeks later Biddle telephoned and said, "I'm sorry, but the position has been offered to a candidate recommended by Isaac Stern." He added that Stern had been so demanding and overbearing that he had had to acquiesce. Biddle then asked if I would be willing to accept the post of deputy director. I thanked him and said that it probably would be best for the music director to select his own person.

Livingston Biddle felt bad, and I had learned a lesson about a kind of power that differs from that of boards of directors. Stern and Leonard Bernstein are arguably *the* worldwide classical music household names of the twentieth century. They both achieved fame and fortune, in addition to power outside their professions. They socialized with the highest-ranking political figures and the aristocracy. Although Stern did save Carnegie Hall (of which he remains president) from the developers, he is infamous among his colleagues for using his power to manipulate people and events for his own benefit. He seems to thrive on controlling every situation in which he is involved.

I sensed then what type of organization the NEA would become. Soon after its inception, staff members were required to do on-site evaluations of grant recipients. After a few years they realized that it was going to be far too heavy a burden to handle in-house, so they subcontracted to Doug Richards, an arts consultant, the task of engaging outside musicians to do the evaluations. Doug once called and asked me to evaluate several orchestras as well as to re-evaluate Arthur Winograd, the music director of the Hartford Symphony Orchestra. Doug confirmed my suspicion that Arthur's first evaluation had been a less-than-good report. I spent three days in Hartford watching Winograd in rehearsal and concert and also talking to the manager and several board members.

I found Arthur, who earlier in life had been a wonderful solo and chamber music cellist, to be a highly competent if not inspiring conductor. I also found the manager and the board to be incompetent. They didn't seem to understand that *they* were the reason the orchestra had financial problems. Even though Hartford is quite a wealthy city, they had not begun to tap its resources. And that is what I wrote in my report to the NEA. It didn't help. The following year Arthur was released. Although the NEA allowed the orchestra board to receive a copy of the report, its guidelines did not allow Arthur to see it. He called me shortly after his dismissal and in his gentlemanly way said that the Hartford board had suggested to him that my report to the NEA was the reason that he was fired. I told Arthur I would gladly send him a copy of what I had given the NEA and that I was being used by his board as a scapegoat for their incompetence. Arthur was understandably bitter about how he had been treated and I was understandably bitter about the ways in which the NEA worked.

Tom Jones (not his real name) is a fine musician who was a valued member of a major orchestra and the EPO for a number of years. Tom had one major problem: he was what we in the business call a "conductor-baiter," someone who constantly questions musical requests of conductors, especially guest conductors, during rehearsals. At EMF musicians repeatedly complained to me about what seemed to them Tom's childish and embarrassing behavior. Because he was such an excellent teacher and player, I was reluctant to release him.

In the late 1970s Tom applied for a position in the music division of the NEA. He had been assured he could continue to perform at EMF and other places while working there. Tom told me to expect a telephone call from an NEA official requesting my recommendation as part of his application process. When I received the call I was honest and said that Tom was a superior musician, diligent and extremely well organized. He got the position.

However, his attitude at EMF worsened and two years later, on the final day of our season, I was approached by several musicians with a petition that said that if I didn't terminate Tom's employment with the Festival they would not return. About two dozen faculty members had signed it. By this point I was in agreement that Tom had to go, and I told him so. His game playing had gotten way out of bounds.

When EMF made their NEA application the following year the news came back that our grant had been cut nearly in half. Our manager, Joyce Beidler, met with our district's congressman, Richardson Preyer, to inquire into the circumstances. Preyer told Joyce that he often saw Liv Biddle (my friend and Jones's superior) on the tennis court and would remind him of his interest in and high regard for EMF. There followed a session in Washington, D.C., at NEA headquarters with Tom, Liv, and Joyce. The upshot was that much of our cut was reinstated. Shortly afterward Tom left the NEA to pursue a conducting career. What astonished me was that *nobody* at the NEA realized what was going on until Congressman Preyer got involved.

In Philadelphia there are two orchestras that are excellent, although certainly not on a par with the Philadelphia Orchestra. The year following EMF's problems with him I was told that Tom had offered one of the two orchestras a promise of an increased NEA allocation in exchange for an opportunity to guest conduct. I also heard that Daniel Webster, the longtime and highly respected chief music critic of the *Philadelphia Inquirer*, had picked up on the incident and written about it.

Recently I contacted Dan to see if there was truth to this. He said he recalled the issue and would attempt to find it in his old files. Dan had recently retired and went to his former office, only to discover that all his materials more than a dozen years old had been destroyed, not even put in the archives. Dan suggested I contact the two conductors. Sidney Rothstein, who had been music director of one of those orchestras and now holds the same position with the Reading Symphony, confirmed the story for me via e-mail. Sid wrote that Jones was indeed the person who made the "offer," although it was made to the other conductor, (whom I'll call conductor X), who refused to allow me to use his name or that of his orchestra.

Conductor X sounded terrified when I telephoned him with my question. He did tell me that although there had been such a "bribe" (his word), it was not from Jones but another wannabe conductor working at the NEA. X said that Jones had indeed guest conducted his orchestra during the time in question and was a good friend.

That Dan and Sid recall it as a Jones ploy and conductor X recalls it as someone else is not important. What is important is that all three acknowledge that it happened and that an NEA employee was involved.

John Frohnmayer, chairman of the NEA for two and a half years before being fired by the first Bush Administration, wrote an interesting book about the NEA's political battles caused by his enemies within the organization as well as those outside it. In his *Leaving Town Alive: Confessions of an Arts Warrior* he describes two particularly interesting episodes.

In one instance Frohnmayer writes about the support he was promised by Senator Nancy Kassebaum just before she voted to cut his budget by 14 percent. Frohnmayer also goes into some detail about his problems with Joe Papp, one of the great American theater producers. Frohnmayer at the time was involved in defending First Amendment rights against attacks from Jesse Helms and his congressional colleagues. Frohnmayer felt that until legislation that would protect artists could be passed, all requests of a controversial nature would have to be put on hold. Papp had been promised a fifty-thousand-dollar NEA grant for a Shakespeare production that included one brief scene with some of the actors in the nude. Because of the larger issues under consideration, the NEA threatened to withdraw his funding. Papp withdrew his application and found the money elsewhere.

In the early 1990s the NEA stopped their on-site evaluations of grant recipients completely, although EMF got in just under the wire. The last person to evaluate the Festival was a private piano teacher from some small city in Tennessee. I have no idea how the NEA found her, but she said we were the greatest thing since sliced bread and we received our last sizeable grant. The NEA then decided to evaluate by other means, including a lengthy five-year plan to be completed by the music directors of orchestras and music festivals. I worked hard on that document, although by that time most NEA grants had been seriously cut or eliminated. The following year the NEA asked that I (and my colleagues around the country) do *another* five-year plan.

One of the best orchestras in the United States did a study recently and realized that when they factored in the number of staff hours required for an NEA application (not to mention the forests cut down), dollar for dollar they would have spent their time more productively raising funds in their own city and forgetting the NEA.

The fact that the NEA has never worked is not surprising. It has confused art with patriotism, and that will never work. From its inception the NEA made it clear that the amount of an orchestra grant would be directly related to the number of American guest artists engaged and the percentage of American music performed—a requirement that smacks of jingoism. What possible reason can the NEA have for trying to determine for music directors which artists they should engage or what they should program? Those being considered as possible music directors are almost always drawn from the ranks of previous guest conductors. NEA's strong suggestion that an orchestra hire Americans to guest conduct, or possibly be penalized with smaller grants, can have a crippling effect, especially on orchestras with smaller budgets, which are in most need of NEA funds. Don't the orchestras deserve the best person for the job of artistic leader? Certainly that is what musicians want and concertgoers deserve. Should musical North America have prevented Rubinstein, Horowitz, or Richter from performing on our stages because they were citizens of other countries? How arrogant to try to put up barriers against the internationality of music. I find little difference between Stalin's attempt to control such artists as Shostakovich and the demands of the NEA (with the important distinction that the NEA never had the power to impose jail terms or conduct executions). Both were concerned with a challenge to the status quo. Shostakovich was silenced for a lengthy period and the NEA has forced U.S. orchestras to perform a great deal of inferior music that concertgoers simply do not want to hear.

◧ THE ARTS HAVE HISTORICALLY RECEIVED FAR FEWER CORporate and foundation contributions than other nonprofit organizations. In an attempt to reverse that trend, citizens in many communities began in 1960 to form arts councils, which work in much the same way as the United Way. They serve as umbrella organizations to which corporations, foundations, and individuals can donate money to be distributed to the member groups. The first arts councils were especially important in smaller communities, where they supported fledgling arts groups that were primarily amateur. In the music world this meant helping sponsor summer bands, pops concerts, and the local symphony orchestra, as well as presenting concerts that appealed to the broadest possible audiences. The buzzword then was "grassroots," and many arts councils excelled in introducing artistic activity to large numbers of people.

But in larger cities they gradually made the mistake of lumping professional and amateur groups together and supporting them equally. Mediocrity was rewarded as much as (or maybe more than) excellence. It is easier to get a bang for the buck with a *Nutcracker* performed by locals than with an evening of Beethoven, Brahms, and Bartók presented by a fully professional orchestra.

Soon the tail began to wag the dog and the councils fell victim to their own bureaucracies. It was reasonable that member groups be restricted in their own fund-raising during the campaigns undertaken by the umbrella organizations. But when those campaigns started lasting two, then four, and finally six months, member groups suffered by not being allowed to approach their own stable of donors for long periods of time. This especially affected the larger, older, and more professional groups, and many, such as the St. Louis Symphony, pulled out.

When the United Arts Council (UAC) of Greensboro began, they begged EMF to join to help give it legitimacy. We agreed in part because at that time there were no restrictions on fund-raising. I have always regretted that decision. The UAC has mostly been feeding its own voracious appetite rather than helping its members. Many arts councils, Greensboro's included, tie grant amounts to the percentage of member groups' board members who contribute to the larger fund. In fact, in its last twenty campaigns during my tenure at EMF, the UAC representative unsubtly hinted to the EMF board that the funds we would receive depended on how much money they individually donated to the UAC! In addition, every member organization that prints a playbill is required to insert several pages listing the names of donors (including the amount of the gift) to UAC—at the organization's expense.

In 1998 the UAC spent more money on running its organization than it distributed to *all* the member groups combined. Less than 70 percent of every dollar raised went to the arts groups. What a waste. Why does EMF stay? Because without a certainty of being able to replace the funds it does receive, the Festival can't afford to leave. It's only 8 percent of the EMF budget, but in our world, every percentage point is crucial.

◈ POPS CONCERTS HAVE LONG BEEN VIEWED AS ESSENTIAL for every orchestra's budget, even though it is a myth that they attract

new classical concertgoers. A few years ago a major North American orchestra gave pops series tickets to a select group of their classical series
ticket buyers and gave classical series tickets to a select group of their pops
series ticket buyers. The goal was to entice more people to purchase
tickets to their classical series. It backfired, and that orchestra lost some
of its classical series audience.

In the heyday of Arthur Fiedler and the Boston Pops Orchestra, pops
concerts were programmed and performed with great dignity and care.
Today's average audience member likely doesn't recognize something
like the blazing last movement of the Tchaikovsky Symphony No. 4 and
other wonderfully melodic gems by great composers that once were standard pops fare. Fiedler on occasion programmed a medley from some
Broadway show, but the majority of his selections were from the classical genre. The pops repertoire has now become so banal and unchal-
lenging (supply and demand requires it) that musicians hate to perform
the concerts. After dancing conductors and low paychecks, nothing de-
moralizes North American musicians more than having to play the boring programs. Many orchestras engage a principal pops conductor and
most union contracts include a clause that allows the principal players
to be excused from those rehearsals and performances.

At EMF three pops concerts are presented each summer, two on location and one in the neighboring city of High Point. The two at EMF
are funded by the county government, and the one in High Point is very
much a social event; all three bring in sorely needed money. Of course,
the very idea of having students take time to rehearse and perform pops
has always offended me as much as having the faculty lose some of their
precious free time. For the board the dollars involved always have out-
weighed the artistic disadvantages, and at EMF I never fought it because
it was a clear no-win situation.

In North America children are often bused in to hear concerts of very
narrow repertoire, such as *Peter and the Wolf,* over and over again. In Geneva in 1994 I saw a poster advertising a youth concert, highly unusual
in Europe, by the Orchestre de la Suisse Romande. The repertoire was
amazing—the Berg Violin Concerto, a twelve-tone composition programmed only with great discretion by most North American music directors. I got a ticket from a good friend in the orchestra, listened to a

man give a three-minute talk about the piece, and watched the faces of the preteen youngsters as they listened to the music in fascination and wonderment. Youth concerts can be useful, but they don't need to include lengthy and preachy speeches or gimmicky music. Far too often we underestimate the intelligence of our young and their innate appreciation for rebels in any discipline.

Pops concerts are designed to appeal to the broadest audience, and in the biggest cities this often means an audience primarily of African American children and their parents. Orchestras going for grants to promote these concerts must show they are somehow relevant to the lives of the audience. Executive and music directors have often responded by engaging African American conductors, promising them the opportunity to conduct more demanding repertoire on a subscription series at some unspecified future date. Many of these conductors get stuck with the pops and children's concert series, losing valuable years conducting insipid music rather than performing the masterpieces. Also, they are often promised that they will move up from an assistant position to associate if things go well, but African Americans have been hearing that tune in almost every area of work for far too long.

SEVENTEEN

What's Next?

IN 2001 THE AVERAGE UNITED STATES CITIZEN IS PAYING
thirty-seven cents per year in taxes directly controlled by the NEA. Think
about it—that's about one-tenth of one cent per day for all those who
are writing, composing, painting, choreographing, and performing what
they see and hear in our culture.

There are many ways to fund the arts and eliminate deficits, the most
effective being sizeable governmental subsidies, though much higher
than the NEA or the Canada Council has ever given. In 1961, when Congress was holding its initial hearings on establishing the NEA, they invited several "name" artists and art lovers to testify, and each person was
asked to name a budget figure that he (women were not involved)
thought would suffice for a beginning. Most gave numbers in the ten-
to twenty-five-million-dollar range. When the esteemed August Heckscher proposed one billion dollars, there was much laughter from the
House panel. Heckscher allowed the guffaws to subside and then said in
his strong but controlled voice, "If I were representing the Pentagon or

the Department of Defense each of you would have taken that suggestion as seriously as I intended and there would have been no laughter."

In fact, however, the Department of Defense does subsidize art, in the form of music—but mostly bad music. Military bands at home and abroad, retained essentially to play anthems, marches, and Johann Strauss waltzes for visiting dignitaries and state occasions, are fully subsidized by U.S. taxpayers in an amount more than double the NEA budget. I recently asked a friend of mine who was in one of those bands what the members did the rest of the time. She responded, "Mostly we sit around and play cards or watch television." And, in a telling statement of government priorities, the budgets of those bands increased in each of the years 1998, 1999, and 2000, during which time Congress was trying to disband the NEA entirely. Art of little or no consequence is subsidized; good art isn't.

Funding priorities both reflect and shape North American attitudes toward the arts. Children attending schools in which arts programs have been eliminated or drastically cut are, by the absence or paucity of such programs, taught that the arts are not worth funding. But athletic programs are, and companies that advertize on mainstream television are fully aware that Michael Jordan and Joe Montana sell, Mozart and Picasso do not. We have become a continent of arts illiterates.

The earlier-mentioned 1965 Rockefeller Panel Report on the performing arts in the United States addresses almost every problem the arts in North America face, and most of it reads as though it could have been written yesterday. The panel recommended arts education in all our public schools, government arts funding on all levels, careful board member selection, and giving artistic directors freedom from intrusion. They warned that if these recommendations were not implemented, our society would be in danger of losing its cultural soul. Today the report is no longer in print. And our cultural soul has become endangered.

The panel's recommendations are necessarily intertwined. As long as there is little or no arts education in our schools, there is no reason for government arts funding of any substance. As long as government subsidies are lacking, board members will be chosen not for their interest or competence in the arts, but for their fund-raising potential. And as long as these people are chosen for their money and social clout, boards will consist of people who want to control how the money is spent, and who think they are entitled to intrude into artistic decisions for which they have no expertise.

As is, North American governments think that if they subsidize the arts, they should be able to dictate. A June 1992 article in the *Chapel Hill Herald* was a reprint of a wonderful satire about the NEA written by the *Providence Journal* columnist Mark Patinkin. It included the following exchange:

> "First applicant," said the NEA chairman.
> "Leonardo Da Vinci."
> "What are you asking funding for?"
> "Please sir," said Leonardo. "A pen and ink drawing I call 'Human Figure in a circle.'"
> The chairman snorted, "You're joking of course, Mr. Da Vinci. You can see his . . . his . . . I won't even say what you can see, but you can see it, and we don't fund this kind of filth." *

When you go into the Rodin Museum in Paris you immediately encounter one of the world's great works of art, "Le Baiser." This sculpture depicts a nude man and woman in an intimate embrace. Most in North America would approve of banning that sculpture from the sight of our schoolchildren. Would NEA have also turned down Rodin? Probably.

Most other governments have a Ministry of Culture that allocates public tax money to the arts. Although these ministries are generally headed by government appointees, knowledge of the arts is requisite. These governments are keeping the arts alive and healthy in their cultures, even though they do not have anything that approaches the wealth of the United States and, to a lesser degree, Canada. The city of Geneva, with a population of 180,000, had an arts subsidy in 1998 of $146 million—almost double the NEA's budget that year for all fifty states and the District of Columbia. In the French village where I live, I, along with all residents of France, pay a small annual tax for the privilege of having a

---

*Mark Patinkin, "Would NEA Turn Down Michelangelo?" *Chapel Hill Herald*, June 1992.

television and radio on which are broadcast theater, ballet, opera, and orchestra productions. The same is true for many other countries. And, as I said in my letter to President-elect Clinton (Appendix II), not just Europe but countries as diverse as Costa Rica, Russia, Japan, and India manage generous subsidies to the arts.

The term "fund-raising" does not translate into French, German, Spanish, or Italian. The concept simply does not exist in non-English speaking countries. A few years ago I discussed with a French conducting colleague the financial plight that North American orchestras face. His response was that it was tough everywhere, that he had to travel three times with his orchestra's manager to the Ministry of Culture in Paris that year just to ensure the standard increase in governmental subsidies for his orchestra.

In contrast, North America has mostly left arts funding to private organizations, and that pool of money becomes smaller every year. During the 1998 U.S. tax year, charitable giving rose by 11 percent. However, the only areas that showed a *decline*—for the third consecutive year— were the arts and humanities. There no longer is a means of finding out the exact percentage of donations from foundations, corporations, and individuals that go directly to symphony orchestras. Fund-raising umbrella organizations like Giving U.S.A. now lump together all gifts to the humanities and the arts, and their 1997 figure was 8.2 percent for these combined areas. One can only guess at the amount orchestras receive. My guess is less than one-tenth of one percent.

That is not enough to prevent disaster. In the last ten years a number of important orchestras have gone bankrupt or are continually on the brink of doing so. These include those of New Orleans, Vancouver, Tulsa, San Diego, Birmingham, London (Ontario), San Antonio, Denver, Toronto, Oakland, and the Ohio Chamber Orchestra/Cleveland Ballet. And although they are reluctant to discuss it, the Detroit Symphony and even the National Symphony are having serious financial problems. Also, I am told in secrecy by personnel in other orchestras that they face similar prospects. The magnitude of these losses would never be tolerated anywhere but in North America. And they are more intolerable here because they are unnecessary.

As one musician told me, during the 1991–92 season the Cincinnati

Symphony Orchestra found itself more than $8 million in the red, primarily because shortsighted management and board decisions had been made to channel major donations to the endowment fund, even though they didn't have enough money for operating expenses. They were borrowing money to pay the musicians' salaries, which seems to me something akin to giving your paycheck to your broker and charging all your expenses to a credit card. In addition, the musicians' pension fund had not been kept up to date. In a rare show of solidarity, the musicians (including the conductors) and staff worked with the board and management to remedy the situation. A small group of donors, led by the Corbett family, which had long been supporters of the arts in Ohio, gave extremely large gifts, and the musicians and staff agreed to perform and work for five weeks without pay. Also, the board was restructured. The plan worked and the group is on sound financial footing—at least for the time being.

While the Saint Louis Symphony Orchestra was climbing to the top level musically, their budgets were increasingly strained. A press release issued on December 6, 2000, stated, "The Saint Louis Symphony Orchestra has reached the top ranks of symphony orchestras but faces financial difficulties. It has had major operating deficits for most of the past two decades." Up stepped the Jack Taylor family (founders of Enterprise Rent-A-Car) with probably the largest single donation in North American orchestral history—a $40 million matching grant over a period of four years. And the grant was largely without conditions, being earmarked for operations and endowment.

At the end of July 2000 the Eastern Music Festival was faced with a deficit of approximately 25 percent of its total budget. Joe Bryan, entering the office of the board president for the second time, made two wise decisions: restructure the board and appeal to the public for the needed funds. He stipulated that the funds be in hand by September 1 or the operation would shut down permanently. The reaction from the community was enthusiastic and astounding, and the funds were raised.

However, while these examples may seem to be portents for the future, all orchestras must remember that such dramatic turnabouts work only once, as the orchestras of Miami and Oakland realized when their citizens refused to rescue them a second time.

Possible sources of additional funds are as numerous as special prose-cutors in the United States. We could establish something like a value-added tax on an item that would not upset the budget of anyone. For example, North Americans pay about one-third to one-fourth less for gasoline than people in most other countries. A gasoline tax of eight-tenths of one cent per gallon would provide an area of six hundred thou-sand inhabitants with approximately three million dollars annually, cer-tainly a sufficient amount to have a first-class orchestra. And this could be done while exempting from such a tax truckers, taxi drivers, and oth-ers whose livelihood depends on travel.

In 1986 an arts council from a midwestern state asked if I would write a feature article for them for their monthly bulletin on a topic of my choice. I decided to make a comparison—without involving figures from the military, which had been overused at that time. Instead, I called their state's Department of Transportation and asked two questions: "How much does it cost you to build one interstate cloverleaf, and how many did you build last year?" The answers were six million dollars and seven. Six million times seven times fifty states equals over two billion dollars. Might it not be possible for each state to build one fewer clover-leaf a year and distribute those monies saved to the arts? They paid me a hundred dollars for the article, and I heard from them only one other time—when they sent me their next issue, with two pages of letters to the editor, all but one condemning my idea.

Where do we begin? As a music educator as well as a conductor, I cannot help thinking that public education must be our first priority. What North America really needs to do is to inject substantial govern-mental funding into local departments of education, which, in consul-tation with local artists, would once again place arts education in the core curriculum, kindergarten through twelfth grade.

Many colleges and universities spend in excess of a half-million dollars each year so their marching and pep bands can travel to sporting events when the contest is played at another school. In 1978, when the NCAA men's basketball finals were played in Philadelphia, three of the four schools sent their entire pep bands. The exception was the University of Michigan, which has a fine school of music. They sent one guitar player and some amplification equipment. Each time the opposing team's pep band started playing (as loudly as possible), the guitar player would play the Michigan school song and completely drown out the opposition.

Public high schools also waste lots of money on pep and marching bands. The band members spend hours each week during football season practicing how to get to the correct place on the field to spell words like "Go Tigers" or to perform other such nonsense for fans, most of whom are in line outside waiting to buy a piece of pizza and a Coke. What a waste! All any school team needs for musical accompaniment is a good guitar player, who probably already has his or her own amplifiers.

Most North Americans born after 1960 have had little or no classroom instruction, much less participation, in the classical performing arts. Nonetheless, there is no reason why we cannot *now* return to a situation in which opera, ballet, serious theater, and classical music would not be alien. It's called public education, the primary means we have of coming to understand the human experience shared by artists and non-artists.

The arts must be restored to the core curriculum in public schools, foundations must change some of their priorities, our elected officials must see to it that sizeable subsidies are made available without strings attached, and corporations must do much more in terms of sponsorships.

Also, North American board members need to spend less time arguing and meeting and more time raising money. It isn't a glamorous task, but it has to be done if there is to be any orchestral future in North America. Subsidies alone cannot cure all the ills.

Much of what I suggest is far easier said than done. While guest conducting in Budapest in 1985 I was housed in a private apartment on Béla Bartók Street, which reminded me of all the streets in Europe that are named for artists and philosophers. In France, for example, there are very few cities or small towns that do not have a rue Voltaire, avenue Ravel, or something similar. In North America, airports, streets, and concert halls are usually named for either the largest donor or some politician—Avery Fisher Hall, Dulles Airport, and the Kennedy Center. Why don't we have an Aaron Copland Boulevard in major cities, a Glenn Gould Expressway or a Charlie Parker Plaza? Could it possibly have something to do with the lack of value our society places on art and those who practice it?

I hate to think that Calvin Coolidge was altogether correct when he said that the business of the American people is business. Or that most would agree with his statement that if the American citizens want art they should just import it from France. Is the wealthiest nation in the world to be remembered only for Microsoft and McDonald's, shopping malls and sports arenas, Disney World and soap operas?

After a recent concert in Poland, my wife and I had a backstage conversation with a shoe salesman who wanted my autograph. When I asked him how he had acquired such a strong interest in classical music he said, with great passion, "Without music there is no bread." His message is for all of us.

APPENDIX 1

Questionnaire

North American orchestras are classified in each year's edition of *Musical America* in terms of budget. The categories are:

AA $10,000,000 (USA dollars) and above;

A $3,600,000 to $10,000,000;

B $1,050,000 to $3,600,000.

   The following is a questionnaire I mailed in 1998 to presidents, executive directors, or staff members of all North American orchestras classified as AA and A. I sent the same questionnaire to only some of the B orchestras because a number of them are not truly professional, according to my definition; i.e., they do not pay most (if any) of their musicians a sufficient living wage. Most (if not all) of their members must seek additional employment. This is not to say in any way that I don't think B-classified orchestras are less than important. They play a vital role in their communities and are an important outlet for musicians of professional caliber who have not yet been able to obtain positions in AA, A, or high-budget B orchestras. However, the purpose of this book is to look at the state of *professional* classical orchestras in the United States and Canada.

   All questionnaires were sent with an internationally stamped return envelope, which does not carry a city postmark, thus allowing the respondent anonymity if he or she wished.

The questions themselves were an attempt to discover if my personal experiences were much the same as the respondents', or, if not, in what ways they differed. I also wanted to know how others are dealing with the myriad problems that face almost all North American orchestras.

I did learn a great deal from the 44 percent who took the time and effort to complete the questionnaire.

1. For all respondents, the average income from all governmental sources was only 7 percent of total budget.
2. Those orchestras that are performing the least amount of repertoire written in the last fifty years are doing better in box office receipts and donations than their counterparts.
3. Most music directors have little latitude in programming or guest artist selection.
4. Engaging high-fee soloists seems to have no bearing on season ticket sales.
5. There is a wide gap between the three orchestra classifications in terms of percentage of board members who give or secure donations. However, I know that this is not necessarily due to the size of a city. For example, Cleveland and Oakland have approximately the same population. However, Cleveland has a world-class orchestra in stable financial condition and Oakland's went bankrupt several years ago.
6. There is a minuscule representation of musicians on the boards. And musicians have little voice in the selection of music directors.
7. Attendance at board meetings is woefully low.
8. It is clear that retreats are a thing of the past. The responses indicated an average of fewer than one a year.

CLASSICAL ORCHESTRA QUESTIONNAIRE (NORTH AMERICA)
(Please fill in the blanks, underline or use NA where appropriate)

Board of Directors *(excluding staff, ad hoc, ex officio or honorary members)*
1. Our board of directors consists of _____ members.
2. Our board (has, has not) a rule against succession. The term of membership is _____ years. On average, our members serve _____ years.
3. Our board membership includes _____ musicians from our orchestra.
4. Our board of directors meets _____ times per year.
5. Attendance at our board meetings averages _____%.
6. Our executive committee consists of approximately _____ members.
7. Attendance at our executive committee meetings averages _____%.
8. Our board members who give or secure funding:
   above $20,000 annually comprise _____% of our board.
   between $10,000-$19,999 annually comprise _____% of our board.

between $5,000–9,999 annually comprise _____% of our board.
between $1,000–$4,999 annually comprise _____% of our board.
less than $1,000 annually comprise _____% of our board.

9. Our board members who do not donate or secure funding in any amount comprise _____% of our board.

10. Our board has _____ retreat(s) annually. At our last retreat _____% attended.

11. Our board members attend, on average, _____% of our primary classical subscription series.

12. Our board members who purchase season tickets to our primary classical subscription series comprise approximately _____% of our board.

Finances

13. According to the listings used in the *Musical America Directory* my orchestra is classified by the letter _____.

14. Our staff (including the music director and assistant(s)) salaries constitute _____% of our total budget.

15. Our musicians' salaries (excluding all guest artists) constitute _____% of our total budget.

16. Fees and related expenses for our guest artists (including guest conductors) constitute _____% of our total budget.

17. Our per concert ticket sales for our primary classical subscription series thus far are (higher, lower) than for the 1996–97 season.

18. Our season ticket sales for our primary classical subscription series are (higher, lower) than for the 1996–97 season.

19. Monies from all governmental sources comprise approximately _____% of our income.

Music Director

20. Our music director (is, is not) currently a music director and/or principal conductor with at least one other orchestra.

21. Our music director (has, does not have) a local address as his/her primary residence.

22. Our music director (is, is not) contracted to be directly involved in fundraising.

23. Our music director is contracted to conduct _____% of our primary classical subscription series.

24. The selection of our guest artists (is, is not) made solely by our music director.

25. The selection of our guest artists (is, is not) made jointly by our music director in conjunction with a committee from the board.

26. Our music director (is, is not) solely responsible for programming for our primary classical music series.
27. Our orchestra's programming for our primary classical subscription series (is, is not) done jointly by our music director and a board committee.
28. Pre-19th century repertoire programmed on our primary classical subscription series for the current season is approximately _____%.
29. 19th century repertoire programmed on our primary classical subscription series for the current season is approximately _____%.
30. Music composed in the past 50 years represents approximately _____% of the repertoire programmed on our primary classical subscription series for the current season.
31. The last time our orchestra had a music director search _____ musicians from our orchestra were members of the committee.
32. Our music director regularly (attends, does not attend) board meetings.
33. Our music director regularly (attends, does not attend) post-concert receptions.
34. Our music director attends _____ retreat(s) annually.

The questionnaire results that follow were reached by the normally accepted mean system.

Board of Directors	AA	A	B
1. No. of members	64	45	39
2. Has rule against succession	100%	99%	61%
Term of membership	3 years	3 years	3 years
Avg. length of service	9 years	6 years	6 years
3. No. of musicians on board	1.5	1.6	0.8
4. No. of board meetings per year	5	7	8
5. Attendance at board meetings	68%	63%	57%
6. Members on executive committee	20	12	9
7. Attendance at exec. comm. mtgs.	76%	78%	75%
8. Board member funding			
$20,000+/year (% of board)	23.6	11.1	5.3
$10,000–19,999/year (% of board)	11.3	8.5	6.1
$5,000–9,999/year (% of board)	15.8	12.6	9.9
$1,000–4,999/year (% of board)	24.2	41.2	33.1
$1–999/year (% of board)	4.2	19.8	19.7
9. Board members not donating or securing funding	20.9%	6.8%	25.9%
10. No. of retreats annually	0	0.4	0.9
Attendance at last retreat	NA	74%	66%
11. Board attendance at subscription series (% of series)	78	62	81

	AA	A	B
12. Board members who purchase season tickets (% of board)	73	76	83

Finances

	AA	A	B
13. Classification (no. responding)	9	14	30
14. Staff salaries, % of total budget	13	16	19
15. Musicians' salaries, % of total budget	36	42	37
16. Guest artist fees & expenses, % of total budget	11	9	8
17. Per concert sales, '97–98 vs. '96–97, % higher	29	89	65
18. Season ticket sales, '97–98 vs. '96–97, % higher	14	83	74
19. Government monies, % of income	3.71	12.01	5.24

Music Director

	AA	A	B
20. Music director working for other orchestra	57%	63%	57%
21. Music director has local primary residence	57%	49%	74%
22. Music director involved in fund-raising	17%	45%	52%
23. Music director conducts % of primary series	24	62	83
24. Guest artists selected solely by music director	0%	40%	39%
25. Guest artists selected by music director and board committee	0%	22%	22%
26. Programming chosen solely by music director	63%	91%	61%
27. Programming chosen by music director and board committee	0%	27%	17%
28. Percentage of programming pre-19th cent.	12%	16%	16%
29. Percentage of programming from 19th cent.	61%	60%	54%
30. Percentage of programming from last 50 yrs.	14%	15%	22%

	AA	A	B
31. No. of musicians involved in last search	2.5	2.9	2.7
32. Music director attends board meetings	14%	43%	78%
33. Music director attends post-concert receptions	100%	100%	100%
34. No. of retreats music director attends annually	NA	0	.3

Overall Statistics

	AA	A	B	Total
Questionnaires sent	23	32	66	121
Questionnaires returned	9 (39%)	14 (44%)	30 (45%)	53 (44%)

Letter to Bill Clinton

Richard Sklar, a friend involved in the Clinton/Gore transition team, suggested I write a letter to Clinton in December 1992. Sy Rosen (the former executive director of the Philadelphia Orchestra and Carnegie Hall) was in cahoots with me in that attempt, and we were both dreamers enough to think someone would listen. Here is what I wrote:

30 December 1992

President-elect Bill Clinton
The White House
1600 Pennsylvania Avenue
Washington, D.C. 20006

Dear Mr. President-elect,

I write not to ask for any position in your administration, but to urge you to examine the precarious state of the arts in our country. Many of us in arts professions worked diligently for your election, in part because of several encouraging statements you and Vice President–elect Gore made on the subject. We are counting on you to lead us now in re-establishing the arts as a vital resource. Unfortunately, what will no longer work are cosmetic changes such as a simple request of Congress for additional funding or new appointments to the National Council for the Arts or to the National Endowment for the Arts.

As you are aware, professional arts organizations in the United States are declaring bankruptcy (or are on the brink of such) at an alarming rate. Scores of my musician friends from throughout the country suddenly find themselves without work, after successful careers, after years of expensive study and practice, after substantial investments in their instruments, because their orchestras have gone out of business. Will it take the folding of the National Symphony (which, incidentally, has a frighteningly large deficit) before we pay attention? Neither NEA nor such lobbying organizations as the American Symphony Orchestra League are constituted in a way to stop this sad avalanche. Anything even akin to "business as usual" (for example, seeking the "advice" of already established so-called superstars) will only prolong the agony faced now by so many artists. The old methods of annually trying to raise funds from the private sector and fighting over the nickels and dimes from the government don't work any more. I plead for a new vision.

The United States of America (and to a lesser degree, Canada) is the only nation that professes a serious attitude toward art but that does not provide meaningful government subsidy. Alone, without a single ally. Countries as diverse as Costa Rica, Japan, and India subsidize their arts. Even the city of Moscow spends 1% of its budget on the arts (*International Herald Tribune*). But what others do that we do not is only part of my argument.

I strongly believe that art should define the culture of our people as it does in other nations. But today the entertainment industry, using its vast funds, has a disproportionate influence on our culture. Our culture is being defined only by Madonna, to the exclusion of Aaron Copland. Are we to continue to understand ourselves only as a nation of rock stars and soap operas? I suspect that we would agree that art should be of and for the people. But for that to happen, the arts must be lively, plentiful and at least as affordable as, say, going to the movies or a Razorback football game (I well realize that tickets to the latter are scarcer than hen's teeth!). A man who runs a small shop in Poland said to me after a symphony concert I recently conducted there, "Without art, there is no bread." With your leadership, we could make the arts as American as apple pie!

Although time is short, I believe it would be instructive to make a study on how arts subsidies work in other nations. The study should include reactions of citizens in those countries that are using tax monies for these subsidies, and it should be made part of the public debate, using the appropriate congressional committee(s). It is tragic that the discourse regarding Maplethorpe and Serrano never rose above issues of censorship. Nowhere did I see mention of the much more important issue of the ludicrously small NEA budget.

For example, the city of Geneva, Switzerland (population of 155,000), gives its arts organizations an amount that is approximately two-thirds of the *total* annual NEA budget.

In this twilight of the arts here, we must consider concepts and approaches not yet tried in the U.S. It might just be, for instance, that NEA ought to be dismantled and replaced by a ministry of culture, either on the national or state level. Or perhaps all arts funding should be subsumed under the Department of Education. But such decisions could only be recommended and realized after a careful and thoughtful presentation. Clearly none of this can occur without your unwavering support for the project. At stake is nothing less than the continued existence—or not—of U.S.A. art. Future generations will decide if we gave it our best effort.

If you are willing to direct that someone in your administration pursue what I have suggested, I would recommend to you (at my instigation, not his) Mr. Seymour Rosen to produce such a study. Mr. Rosen is the former manager of the Pittsburgh Symphony Orchestra, the Philadelphia Orchestra, artistic director of Carnegie Hall—impeccable credentials, and perhaps the most respected management person in the American performing arts field. He is currently the Dean of the School of Fine Arts at Arizona State University, and he plans to accept his late retirement but never to stop in his quest for finding a comprehensive means of solidifying support for the world of art nationwide.

I am certainly not the first person to show such a passionate concern about this issue, and because much of my career has been spent conducting orchestras in Europe as well as America, I have long been aware of the inadequacies of arts subsidies in my country. But the Rockefeller Brothers Fund report of nearly three decades ago forecast the present situation, and they were so directly on target that their report could just as well have been written yesterday. Also, in the mid-sixties, Fredrich Dorian (who had worked extensively with Brecht and Weill in Europe) made an extensive study not unlike the one I now propose. His proposals also were on target. Yet neither of these excellent studies would be pertinent in today's climate. A fresh approach is mandatory, lest we soon find ourselves as the wealthiest nation on earth which claims it cannot afford to provide its citizens access to creative self-expression on the highest level.

I realize this is a lengthy document, longer than I had intended. But what is at issue is too vital to be dismissed lightly at this moment in our nation's history. I thank you for your consideration and would welcome your response.

Sheldon Morgenstern
Music Director
Eastern Music Festival

The response was a printed postcard:

Dear Mr. Morgenstern:
Thank you for your interest in our new administration. We will certainly consider your suggestion.

Bill Clinton [signature stamped]

Select Bibliography

Anderson, Emily. *The Letters of Mozart.* London: Macmillan, 1938.

Bouton, Jim. *Ball Four.* New York: Macmillan, 1970.

Cowen, Arthur. *Artists and Enemies.* Boston: David R. Godine, 1987.

Damrosch, Walter. *My Musical Life.* New York: Charles Scribner's Sons, 1940.

Daniels, David. *Orchestral Music.* Lanham, Md.: Scarecrow Press, 1996.

Dufourca, Norbert. *La Musique: les hommes; les instruments; les oeuvres.* Paris: Auge, Gillon, Hollier-Larousse, Moreau, 1965.

Fassett, Agatha. *The Naked Face of Genius.* Boston: Riverside Press, 1958.

Frohnmayer, John. *Leaving Town Alive: Confessions of an Arts Warrior.* Boston: Houghton Mifflin, 1993.

Giving USA. *AAFRC Trust for Philanthropy.* New York, 1998.

Gould, Glenn. "Let's Ban Applause!" *Musical America* (February 1962): 245–47.

Grout, Donald Jay. *A History of Western Music.* New York: W. W. Norton, 1960.

Holland, Bernard. "Making Music by Sleight of Hand and Eye." *New York Times,* August 13, 1995, Arts and Leisure section.

Lebrecht, Norman. *When the Music Stops.* London: Simon & Schuster, 1997.

Lipman, Samuel. *Music after Modernism.* New York: Basic Books, 1979.

McCarthy, Eugene. *Up 'Til Now.* New York: Harcourt Brace Jovanovich, 1987.

Morgenstern, Sheldon. *Wolf Trap Farm Park Report.* Washington, D.C.: United States Department of the Interior, 1967.

Musical America. *International Directory of the Performing Arts.* Hightstown, N.J.: Promedia, 1999.

Ostwald, Peter. *Glenn Gould: The Ecstacy and Tragedy of Genius.* New York: W. W. Norton, 1997.

Patinkin, Mark. "Would NEA Turn Down Michelangelo?" *Chapel Hill Herald,* June 1992.

Prausnitz, Frederik. *Score and Podium.* New York: W. W. Norton, 1983.

Rockefeller Panel Report. *The Performing Arts: Problems and Prospects.* New York: McGraw-Hill, 1965.

Schuller, Gunther. *The Compleat Conductor.* New York: Oxford University Press, 1997.

Shostakovich, Dmitri. *Testimony.* New York: Harper & Row, 1979.

Toffler, Alvin. *The Culture Consumers.* Toronto: Macmillan, 1964.

Index